Hindi Urdu BOL CHAAL

اُردُو

A Beginners' Course in Spoken Hindi and Urdu on BBC Television

हिन्दी

CENTRE FOR CONTINUING EDUCATION
UNIVERSITY OF EDINBURGH
11 BUCCLEUCH PLACE
EDINBURGH EH8 9LW
SCOTLAND

Course Writers
Mangat Bhardwaj, Handsworth College
Gordon Wells, Kilmarnock College

Language and Background Consultant
Nazir-ul-Haq, Handsworth College

Producer
Jeremy Orlebar

اُردُو

Hindi Urdu

BOL
CHAAL

A Beginners' Course in Spoken Hindi and Urdu on BBC Television

हिन्दी

BBC BOOKS

Hindi Urdu Bol Chaal is a course for beginners in spoken Hindi and Urdu on BBC Television, first broadcast in October 1989 (produced by Jeremy Orlebar).

The course consists of:
10 television programmes
This course book covering all the programmes
Two audio cassettes

This book is published to accompany a series of programmes prepared in consultation with the BBC Educational Broadcasting Council.

Cover illustration: print Cedric reproduced by permission of Liberty of London prints.

Published by BBC Books
A division of BBC Enterprises Ltd
Woodlands, 80 Wood Lane, London W12 0TT

First published 1989
Reprinted 1989 and 1990

© BBC Enterprises Limited 1989

ISBN 0 563 21456 2

This book is set in 10 on 12 point Bembo
by Ace Filmsetting Ltd, Frome, Somerset
Printed and bound in Great Britain by
Richard Clay Ltd, Norwich, Norfolk

Contents

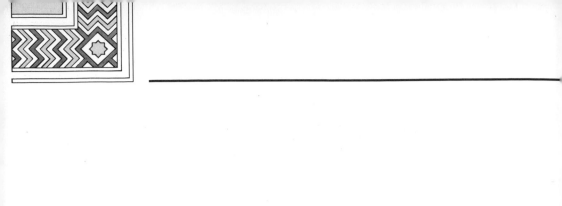

Introduction

THE COURSE

Welcome to **Hindi Urdu Bol Chaal**, the course that introduces you to two languages at once. **Bol Chaal** means 'talk' or 'conversation', and **Hindi Urdu Bol Chaal** is a course which teaches you everyday *spoken* Hindi and Urdu – the kind of language you can use in ordinary conversation with friends, relations, neighbours or working colleagues. It's a course for beginners – no previous knowledge of either Hindi or Urdu (or any other South Asian language) is assumed – and it starts with a gentle introduction to the language for a range of common day-to-day purposes and topics to do with family, friends and food. Later, in the second half, the course picks up pace and covers in some detail a variety of other more specialised subjects such as travel, leisure, health and education.

But how can you learn two languages at once? One thing you'll learn as you go through this course is something about the background and history of Hindi and Urdu – both in Britain and in South Asia – and you'll see that the two languages have a lot in common. Although they have different scripts, and quite different vocabularies in many areas, they share the same basic grammar and pronunciation. So, for a learner who wants a basic introduction to the spoken language it's quite feasible to tackle both together. Hopefully, once you've started learning to speak, you'll go on to learn one or both of the scripts as well, though you don't need either to complete this course.

And you won't need to go to India or Pakistan to use the Hindi and Urdu you learn. They are both living languages here in Britain, and it shouldn't be difficult to find opportunities to practise as soon as you start learning. Good luck!

THE TELEVISION PROGRAMMES

Each programme introduces you to some new language to do with a particular topic. You'll see and hear how Hindi and Urdu are used up and down Britain, from London to Birmingham, to Bradford and Glasgow. The programmes will include stories illustrating the lives of Hindi and Urdu speakers and the part the languages play in social, business and family life. They will also regularly feature students studying the languages and practising what they have learnt.

THE BOOK

The book has ten units, dealing in more detail with the material introduced in the corresponding television programme. Each unit has the following sections:

DIALOGUES AND NOTES

A selection of dialogues illustrating key teaching points for that unit. Each dialogue is accompanied by notes which explain the structure and meaning of any new material. These sections feature a special dual translation system. Directly underneath the Hindi and Urdu a *word for word* translation is given. The translation that appears to the right (sometimes below right) of the Hindi and Urdu gives the closest equivalent of what the sentence means *in the context in which it is used* in *ordinary, natural* English. The *word for word* translation helps you to identify the *individual words* and how they combine with each other. You'll see that sometimes the *word for word* translations are quite different from the *natural* ones – sometimes there is no real English equivalent at all for a Hindi or Urdu word and vice versa. The dual translation system helps you to compare Hindi and Urdu with English and note for yourself points of similarity and difference.

The fact that in places they are quite *different* doesn't have to make Hindi and Urdu *difficult* for you. If you can see how Hindi and Urdu grammar works in its own way, rather than trying to force it into an English grammatical framework, then you'll really get a true feeling for the languages and make quick progress.

CHECK-UP

A quick check at the end of each dialogue and notes section to make sure you've understood.

KEYWORDS

This section gives all the Hindi and Urdu words taught in the unit in the order in which they're introduced.

SOUND SYSTEMS

A simple explanation of a particular pronunciation point which may cause an English speaker some difficulty.

HOW THE LANGUAGE WORKS

Explanations of Hindi and Urdu grammar relating to new material in the dialogues. This section gives a broader picture of the structure of the languages than the notes.

EXERCISES

A series of exercises which gives you the chance to practise what you've learnt. Each unit contains an extra listening exercise, and one other exercise you can use to practise listening and speaking.

BACKGROUND

Information about Hindi and Urdu and how they are used, with some tips for learners on how to use resources around you to help you learn more.

REVIEW SECTIONS

As well as the ten units there are also two review sections, one halfway through, and one at the end of the book, which offer you the option of extra listening practice. Review 1 comes after Unit 5 and contains a questionnaire so you can check what you should have learnt by that stage. It also contains a series of short listening exercises which you can use selectively to brush up your weaker points. Review 2 is a long listening passage which brings together points from all ten units.

GUIDE TO PRONUNCIATION

An explanation of the system used to represent Hindi and Urdu sounds in Roman letters, and tips on how to make unfamiliar sounds.

GRAMMATICAL SUMMARY

A summary of the grammar of Hindi and Urdu covered in Units 1–10.

EXERCISE KEY

Answers to all check-ups and exercises in Units 1–10 and Review 1.

WORD GROUPS

Additional vocabulary lists organised under topic headings in English with Hindi and Urdu equivalents.

VOCABULARY

A list of all the Hindi and Urdu words that appear in the units and reviews with English translations.

LISTENING EXERCISE TRANSCRIPTS

All the passages used for the listening exercises in Units 1–10 and in Review 1.

THE AUDIO CASSETTES

On the cassettes that go with this book there is a separate section corresponding to each unit and the reviews. They contain the dialogues as well as exercises for listening and speaking, and 'sound systems' pronunciation practice.

HOW TO USE THIS COURSE

Different people like to learn languages in different ways, and there is no one right way. The right way to learn is really the one that works for *you*. So don't feel you have to go through this book page by page from front to back, though you can certainly do that if you want. Think of it as one of a number of resources alongside the cassettes and the television programmes which you can use in the way you choose and that best supports your own learning style.

Some people, for example, like to understand all the grammatical rules of the language they're learning as it helps them to cope with new and different structures. If you're like that you'll find 'How the language works' and the dual translation system helpful. Other people feel they learn better if they get lots of practice in hearing the language in use. They might prefer to spend more time listening to the cassettes and watching the television programmes several times. You may want to experiment for a while before deciding on your own balance of learning activities and settling into a rhythm.

It probably helps, though, to establish a regular weekly routine, so that you set aside certain times of the day to concentrate on **Hindi Urdu Bol Chaal**. Be sure to give yourself enough time too, and bear in mind that the second half of the course picks up the learning pace, so you'll probably need to commit more time after Unit 5.

You can prepare for the television programmes by reading through the book units first. Go through the dialogues and notes and learn the keywords. That way you'll be ready for the new language when you hear it on the programme. 'How the language works' will also help you understand the structure of new sentences you learn. And if you want to take it further have a look at the grammatical summary.

You don't need to do all the exercises in one go, and you can check your answers on one before going on to the next. You don't have to leave the background information to last either. Have a look at it any time you need a short break from language learning!

You'll need the cassette tapes in order to do the listening exercises in each unit and in the reviews. They will also be helpful to practise your pronunciation along with 'sound systems' in the book. In fact, the tapes are worth listening to any time you have a spare minute at home or in the car. The more Hindi and Urdu you hear the more you get accustomed to the sounds and the less strange they seem. Try making them yourself. Get a blank tape and record yourself doing some dialogue either on your own, or with a friend who's learning.

Best of all, find someone who already speaks Hindi or Urdu and who's prepared to help you learn. Ask them to demonstrate sounds or practise dialogues with you. Pretty soon you'll be having real conversations!

kyaa haal hai?

MEETING AND GREETING PEOPLE

SAYING WHO YOU ARE

 1

Hindi and Urdu greetings are chosen not according to the time of day (like English 'Good morning' and 'Good afternoon'), but according to the religion of the speakers. Here are some people greeting each other:

Sneh:	**namaste.**
Manmohan Ram:	**namaste.**
Omar:	**assalaam alaikum.**
Javad Iqbal:	**vaalaikum assalaam.**
Sneh:	**sat srii akaal.**
Darshan Singh:	**sat srii akaal.**

NOTES

namaste is the Hindu greeting. It's taken from Sanskrit and literally means 'I greet you respectfully'. The reply is also **namaste**. **jii** can be added, as it can be to many words, to show additional respect: **namaste jii**. To say 'Goodbye' the same word **namaste** is used.

The Muslim greeting is **assalaam alaikum**, which is taken from Arabic and means 'Peace be on you'. The reply is **vaalaikum assalaam**, which means 'Peace be on you also'. There is a different phrase for 'Goodbye' – **Khudaa haafiz**.

The Sikh greeting is **sat srii akaal**, which comes originally from Sanskrit and means 'The truth (or God) is eternal'. Like **namaste** it is used both on meeting and parting.

When people from different religious communities greet *each other*

there are *no* hard and fast rules as to which is the most appropriate greeting to use. Depending on how well you know the other person, and how friendly you are towards them you may or may not wish to use their religious greeting. If unsure, or if you don't know what their religion is, then just say 'hello' or 'hello **jii**'.

CHECK-UP 1 Why did Sneh (a Hindu) say **sat srii akaal** to Darshan Singh, instead of **namaste** or **assalaam alaikum**?

2

When you meet someone, you don't just say hello. You ask how they're getting on:

Ambar:	Hello **jii**.
Naveed:	Hello **jii**.
Ambar:	**kyaa haal hai?**
Naveed:	**Thiik hai. kyaa haal hai?**
Ambar:	**Thiik hai.**
Sneh:	Omar **jii, aap kaise hãĩ?**
Omar:	**mãĩ Thiik hũũ. aap kaisii hãĩ?**
Sneh:	**mãĩ bhii Thiik hũũ.**

NOTES

To make a general enquiry you say:

aapkaa kyaa haal	**hai?**	How are you getting on?,
your what condition is		How are things?

Very often **aapkaa** is left out because it is understood, so you simply say **kyaa haal hai?**

To say you're doing fine in reply you can say:

Thiik hai	Fine
(condition) fine is	

haal is left out because it is understood.

To ask how someone is feeling:

aap kaise/kaisii hãi?   How are you?, How are you
you   how   are   feeling?

kaise is the masculine form and is used when talking to a man. When talking to a woman use the feminine form, **kaisii**.

To say you are feeling fine:

mãi Thiik hũu   I'm fine
I   fine   am

Again **mãi** can be left out because it's understood, so you can just say **Thiik hũu**. If you want to say 'I'm fine *too*' you need an extra word **bhii** after **mãi**:

mãi bhii Thiik hũu   I'm fine too
I   also   fine   am

CHECK-UP 2 Does Ambar want to know how Naveed is feeling, or is she making a more general enquiry?

3

If you're meeting someone for the first time you'll want to find out their name. And you'll want to tell them yours:

Sneh:	**aapkaa naam kyaa hai?**
Darshan Singh:	**meraa naam** Darshan Singh **(darshan singh) hai.**
Sneh:	**meraa naam** Sneh **hai. aapkaa naam kyaa hai?**
Harbans:	**meraa naam** Harbans **(harbans) hai.**
Sneh:	**namaste.**
Manmohan Ram:	**namaste.**
Sneh:	**aapkaa naam kyaa hai?**
Manmohan Ram:	**meraa naam** Manmohan Ram **(manmohan raam) hai.**

NOTES

If you want to ask someone's name you say:

aapkaa naam kyaa hai?   What's your name?
your   name   what is

And they might reply:

meraa naam Sneh **hai.**   My name is Sneh.
my   name   Sneh is

CHECK-UP 3 Sneh tells her name to only one of the people she speaks to. Which one?

KEYWORDS

△	**namaste**	Hindu greeting
△	**assalaam alaikum**	Muslim greeting
△	**vaalaikum assalaam**	Reply to Muslim greeting
△	**Khudaa haafiz**	Muslim farewell
△	**sat srii akaal**	Sikh greeting
△	**jii**	Mark of respect like Sir or Madam (though less formal)
△	**kyaa**	what?
△	**haal** (m)	condition
△	**hai**	is
△	**Thiik**	fine
△	**aap . . . haĩ**	you are . . .
△	**maĩ . . . hũũ**	I am . . .
△	**kaise/kaisii**	how
△	**bhii**	also, too
△	**aapkaa**	your
△	**naam** (m)	name
△	**meraa**	my

SOUND SYSTEMS

~/˜ THE SIGN OF NASALISATION

There are ten basic vowels in Hindi and Urdu (see *Guide to Pronunciation*). However, there are two distinct ways of pronouncing each one of them – either just through the mouth or through the mouth and nose together. If they're pronounced in the second way – 'nasalised' – they're written with this sign ~/˜ over the top. It's not difficult to produce a nasalised vowel once you know how. Although we don't do it much in English, if you can pronounce the French *bon* or *pain* you can do it already. It's important to try. Remember **hai** and **haĩ** are two *different* words ('is' and 'are' respectively).

HOW THE LANGUAGE WORKS

WORD ORDER

Unlike English, the order of words in a Hindi or Urdu sentence is not rigidly fixed. You will often hear **aapkaa kyaa naam hai?** as an alternative to **aapkaa naam kyaa hai?** for instance, with no real difference in meaning. This does not mean that you can 'put anything anywhere'. One major difference compared with English is the position of the *verb*. A word for word translation of **mãĩ Thiik hũũ** gives 'I fine *am*', the word for 'am', **hũũ**, coming at the end of the sentence instead of in the middle as in English 'I *am* fine'. The general pattern is for all Hindi and Urdu verbs to come at the end of the sentence.

IS, AM, AND ARE

Just as in English it is considered wrong to say 'you am', or 'they is', so in Hindi and Urdu you have to choose between **hãĩ** and **hai** and **hũũ** according to whom you are talking about, 'they' or 'she' or 'I' etc:

mãĩ hũũ	I am
tuu hai	You are (very familiar)
ye*/vo** hai	This/that is
ham hãĩ	We are
tum ho	You are (familiar)
ye/vo*** hãĩ	These/those are
aap hãĩ	You are (polite)

* Formal and written Hindi **yah**
** Formal and written Hindi **vah**
*** Formal and written Hindi **ve**

Don't worry too much about all the different words for 'you' at this stage. It's as well to know that they exist, but in your own usage you will be quite safe if you stick to **aap**. This is actually a plural form, but you use it, like French *vous*, when speaking to one person as well in order to be polite.

We'll start using **ye** and **vo** in Units 3 and 4.

EXERCISES

1
Starting up
What would you say in these situations?
- *a* You bump into a Hindu friend in the street.
- *b* You meet a Muslim friend in a sweet centre for lunch.
- *c* You're introduced to a Hindi or Urdu speaker but you don't know what their religion is.
- *d* You meet a stranger at a friend's house. You don't know her name.
- *e* You meet a friend you haven't seen for a couple of days. You wonder how he is.
- *f* A friend introduces you to a Sikh acquaintance of hers.

2
Answering back
How would you reply to someone who said this to you?
- *a* **assalaam alaikum**
- *b* **kyaa haal hai?**
- *c* **namaste**
- *d* **aapkaa naam kyaa hai?**
- *e* **aap kaise/kaisii hãĩ?**
- *f* Hello **jii**
- *g* **sat srii akaal**

3
How did it start?
How did the conversation begin in each of these situations?

4
Is, am and are

Choose a word from the right hand column to complete the sentences.

a	aapkaa naam kyaa _____?	hũ̃
b	aapkaa kyaa haal _____?	hai
c	mãĩ Thiik _____	hãĩ
d	aap kaise _____?	

5
Word search

This square contains at least ten of the words used in this chapter (see *Keywords* p. 16). You can read up or down, left or right, and you can add a ~ anywhere you like. See how many you can find in two minutes.

```
e  s  i  a  k  a
t  a  a  r  y  l
s  l  p  l  a  a
a  a  k  p  a  a
m  a  i  a  b  r
a  m  i  a  h  e
n  e  h  a  i  m
a  r  T  i  i  j
```

6
Crossword

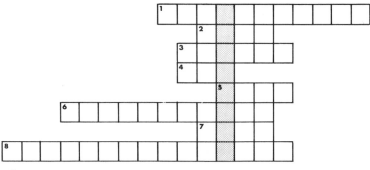

Clues:

1 I'm fine	4 is	7 name
2 also	5 what	8 greeting
3 how	6 how are you?	

What's the phrase written vertically in the darker boxes?

7
Listening exercise
Listen to the short conversation on the tape. Listen for the greetings:
are they Hindu, Sikh or Muslim? What are the names of the two
people? How are they?

8
Fill in the gaps
A **assalaam alaikum**
B **vaalaikum assalaam**
A **meraa naam** Raab Nawaz _____. _____ **naam kyaa hai?**
B _____ **naam** Pir Mohammed **hai**
A **aapkaa** _____ **haal hai?**
B **Thiik** _____ **aap kaise** _____?
A **mãĩ** _____ **Thiik hũũ.**

BACKGROUND

HINDI AND URDU AND THE INDO-EUROPEAN LANGUAGE FAMILY

One way of looking at languages is to divide them up into families.
Most people know, for instance, that Spanish and Portuguese are
closely related. They have a common 'parent', or perhaps 'grand-
parent' language, Latin, so they belong to the family of Romance
languages along with Italian and French and several others. The
Romance languages in turn are part of a larger 'extended family'. We
know that they are more distantly related to the Germanic languages
such as Swedish, German, and English too. This extended family
spreads far beyond the boundaries of Europe, and is usually called the
Indo-European family of languages. Urdu and Hindi belong to this
same extended family so we can actually think of them as being
distant cousins of English (a few times removed). Hindi and Urdu,
along with Punjabi, Gujarati, Bengali and many other North Indian
languages have a common ancestor in Sanskrit, a classical Indian
language as old as Ancient Greek. (See the 'family tree' overleaf.)

This is not the whole story however. Languages borrow from other
languages, and, while Hindi and Urdu come from the same source
language, Urdu has borrowed heavily from Arabic and Persian. Not
only is the script borrowed from Arabic (which is not an Indo-European language) but also a large number of words. Hindi on the other
hand has taken its script and a large number of words directly from
Sanskrit.

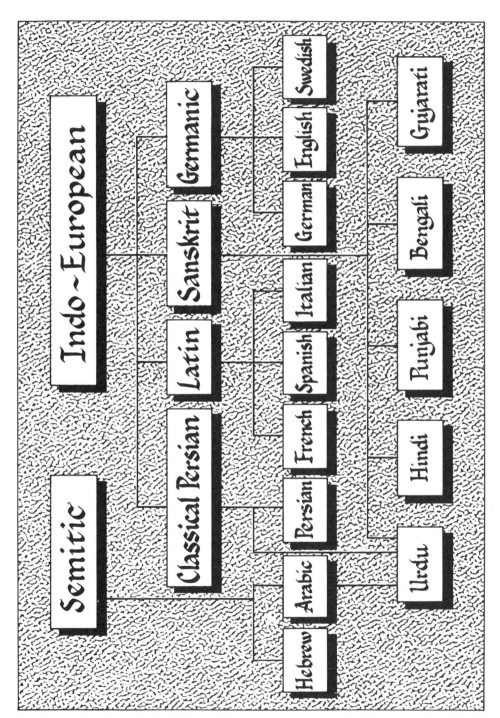

aap kyaa kaam karte hãĩ?

TALKING ABOUT YOURSELF AND YOUR JOB

TALKING ABOUT PLACES AND TRANSPORT

 1

You now know how to greet people, and to ask how they are. You also know how to ask their names and tell them yours. You may want to tell them more about yourself, about your job or where you live. Anita Bhalla talked to people living and working in and around Birmingham:

Anita:	**namaste jii.**
Dr Shah:	**namaste jii.**
Anita:	**aapkaa naam kyaa hai?**
Dr Shah:	**meraa naam** Minesh Shah **(minesh shaah) hai.**
Anita:	**aap kyaa kaam karte hãĩ?**
Dr Shah:	**mãĩ ĐaakTar hũũ.**

Anita:	**assalaam alaikum.**
Rena Azim:	**vaalaikum assalaam.**
Anita:	**aap kaisii hẫi?**
Rena Azim:	**mẫi Thiik hũũ. aap kaisii hẫi?**
Anita:	**mẫi bhii Thiik hũũ. aap kahẫã rahtii hẫi?**
Rena Azim:	**mẫi** Bordesley Green **mẽ rahtii hũũ.**

NOTES

If you want to ask someone about his or her job you can say:
aap kyaa kaam karte/kartii hẫi?
you what work　　doing　are
　　　　　　　　　　　　What is your job?

If you want to ask them about where they live, say:
aap kahẫã rahte/rahtii hẫi?　Where do you live?
you where　living　are

The difference between **karte** and **rahte** on the one hand and **kartii** and **rahtii** on the other is the same as that between **kaise** and **kaisii** which we came across in Unit 1. **karte** and **rahte** are masculine; **kartii** and **rahtii** are feminine. Use these masculine forms for addressing men and the feminine forms for women, whenever you use **aap**.

If you want to tell someone what your job is, you can say:
mẫi DaakTar hũũ　　　　　I am a doctor
I　doctor　am

And to tell someone where you live, say:
mẫi Bordesley Green **mẽ rahtii/rahtaa hũũ**
I　Bordesley Green　-in　　living　am
　　　　　　　　　　　　　I live in Bordesley Green

With **mãĩ** you use **rahtaa** if you are a man, and **rahtii** if you are a woman.

CHECK-UP 1 What is the doctor's full name?

2

Sometimes you want to know more precisely where someone lives:

Anita:	**aap kahãã rahte hãĩ?**
Dr Shah:	Birmingham **mẽ.**
Anita:	Birmingham **mẽ kahãã?**
Dr Shah:	Moseley **mẽ**, Emsbury Ŕoad **par.**

At the neighbourhood office Javad Iqbal noted down a client's details:

Javad:	**aap kahãã rahtii hãĩ?**
Vijay:	**mãĩ** Sutton **mẽ rahtii hũũ.**
Javad:	Sutton **mẽ kahãã?**
Vijay:	Lichfield Road **par.**

NOTES

If you want to ask *where* in a particular place, say:
Birmingham **mẽ kahãã?**   Where in Birmingham?
Birmingham -in where

You may want to say *on* a particular road in your reply:
Emsbury Road **par**   On Emsbury Road
Emsbury Road -on
Take care that the words for 'in' and 'on' come *after*, not *before* the place name.

CHECK-UP 2 Where does Vijay live?

3

These people live away from their work. Anita talked to bus driver Resham Singh Heer at the bus depot:

Anita:	**aap kahãã rahte hãĩ?**
Resham:	**mãĩ** Handsworth Wood **mẽ rahtaa hũũ.**
Anita:	Handsworth Wood **mẽ kahãã?**
Resham:	Underwood Road **par.**
Anita:	**aap** Handsworth Wood **se yahãã kaise aate hãĩ?**
Resham:	**mãĩ kaar mẽ aataa hũũ.**

Javad asked Vijay some more questions in the neighbourhood office:

Javad:	**aap kahãã kaam kartii hãĩ?**
Vijay:	**mãĩ** Edgbaston **mẽ kaam kartii hũũ.**
Javad:	**aap vahãã kaise jaatii hãĩ?**
Vijay:	**mãĩ bas mẽ jaatii hũũ.**

NOTES

If you want to ask how someone comes *here*, you can say:

aap (Handsworth Wood **se)   yahãã kaise aate/aatii hãĩ?**
you Handsworth Wood -from here   how   coming   are
                              How do you come here (from
                              Handsworth Wood)?

And to say how you come, use:
mãĩ kaar mẽ aataa/aatii hũũ   I come by car
I   car   -in   coming   am

If you need to ask where someone works, say:
aap kahãã kaam kartii/karte hãĩ?
you where work   doing   are
                              Where do you work?

If you want to ask how someone goes *there*:
aap vahãã kaise jaatii/jaate hãĩ?
you there   how   going   are
                              How do you go there?

As with **rahtaa/rahte/rahtii**, you again have to choose from **aataa/aate/aatii** and from **jaataa/jaate/jaatii** according to whether you're using it with **aap** (plural) or **mãĩ** (singular) and to the gender (or whether the person concerned is a man or a woman). **kaise**, however, does not change here for gender, because it refers to the *manner* of travelling and not to any person or thing.

Look at the words which describe the position of someone or something:

Handsworth Wood **mẽ**	*In* Handsworth Wood
Underwood Road **par**	*On* Underwood Road
Handsworth Wood **se**	*From* Handsworth Wood

'In', 'on', and 'from' all come *before* the name of the place. They are called *pre*positions in English. However, their equivalents in Hindi and Urdu – **mẽ, par,** and **se** come *after* the placename. They are *post*positions. This is an important difference between English, and Hindi and Urdu. Always remember to put the Hindi and Urdu equivalents of English *pre*positions *after* the word to which they refer and not before.

CHECK-UP 3 How does Vijay go to work?

KEYWORDS

△	**kaam** (m)	work, job
△	**kar**	do
△	**kartaa/karte/kartii**	doing
△	**DaakTar** (m/f)	doctor
△	**kahãã**	where?
△	**rah**	live, dwell
△	**rahtaa/rahte/rahtii**	living, dwelling
△	**mẽ**	in
△	**par**	on
△	**yahãã**	here
△	**aa**	come
△	**aataa/aate/aatii**	coming
△	**kaar** (f)	car
△	**vahãã**	there
△	**jaa**	go
△	**jaataa/jaate/jaatii**	going
△	**bas** (f)	bus
△	**Tren** (f)	train
△	**ko**	to
△	**jaan**	know
△	**jaantaa**	knowing
△	**dukaandaar** (m/f)	shopkeeper
△	**Tiichar** (m/f)	teacher
△	**nars** (m/f)	nurse
△	**bas Draaiivar** (m/f)	bus driver
△	**vakiil** (m/f)	lawyer

SOUND SYSTEMS

a AND ah

Single **a** in Hindi and Urdu is not like the English 'a' in 'hat' or 'gas'. It is quite a 'central' vowel, being pronounced more or less in the middle of the mouth, more like the 'u' in a southern English pronunciation of 'but' or the 'a' in 'about'. That's why the English loanword 'bus' is spelt **bas**. **a** nearly always has this pronunciation, unless it is followed by **h**, as in **rahtaa** or **rahtii**. When **a** is followed by **h** and then another consonant or **a** again, then it sounds more like the **ai** in **hai**.

HOW THE LANGUAGE WORKS

VERB STEMS

The *Keywords* section of this unit lists the new verbs you have learnt – words for 'go', 'do' etc. They are listed in two ways – as *stem* forms like **jaa** and **kar**, and also with endings like **jaataa, jaatii** or **karte.** The stem form is the most basic form of any verb to which endings like **-taa**, and others you will learn in later units, are added. Normally any new verbs will be listed in *Keywords* in their stem form.

AN 'ONGOING SITUATION' – THE HINDI AND URDU -taa FORM

The Hindi and Urdu **-taa** form, a bit like the English '-ing' form, is added to a verb stem to refer to an *ongoing* and *uncompleted* activity or happening. So, if you ask someone **aap kahãã kaam kar*te* hãĩ?**, or **aap kahãã rah*tii* hãĩ?** you're assuming that they're still work*ing* or liv*ing* somewhere. The **-taa** form is not always best translated as -*ing* however. Because it can also refer to a *habitual* activity or a *mental state of affairs* (unlike English '-ing') it is often better translated into English 'simple present' tense:

mãĩ Tren mẽ jaatii hũũ	I go by train.
I train -in going am	

mãĩ Muhammad Ali **ko jaantaa hũũ**	
I Muhammad Ali -to knowing am	
	I know Muhammad Ali.

The **-taa** form changes to agree in *number* and *gender* with the person you are talking about – the *subject* of the sentence. (Remember from Unit 1 that **aap** is plural in order to be polite even if you are talking to one person):

Resham:	**mãĩ kaar mẽ aataa hũũ.**	(Masculine Singular)
Rena:	**mãĩ** Bordesley Green **mẽ rah*tii* hũũ.**	(Feminine Singular)
Anita:	(to Dr Shah) **aap kyaa kaam kar*te* hãĩ?**	(Masculine Plural)
Javad:	(to Vijay) **aap vahãã kaise jaa*tii* hãĩ?**	(Feminine Plural)

These are the shapes the **-taa** form takes:

	Masculine	Feminine
Singular (e.g. **mãĩ**, 'I')	**-taa**	**-tii**
Plural (e.g. **aap**, 'you')	**-te**	**-tĩĩ***

* **-tĩĩ** becomes **-tii** when it is followed by **hãĩ**, as in all the examples we have seen so far.

ENGLISH WORDS IN HINDI AND URDU

It is common for speakers of Hindi and Urdu, especially in Britain, to make use of English words in their daily speech. You will see from the *Keywords* section of this unit that a number of common job titles, for example, are taken from English. The pronunciation of these words is quite often changed. The way they are spelt shows how they are commonly pronounced by many speakers. However, you will find a lot of variety in their pronunciation from speaker to speaker. Don't feel you should try to change your own natural pronunciation of these words when you use them in Urdu or Hindi.

EXERCISES

1

Who's who?

Fill in the empty name plates

a **meraa naam** Chandubhai Patel **hai.
mãĩ dukaandaar hũũ.**

b **meraa naam** Afzal Chaudhari **hai.
mãĩ Tiichar hũũ.**

c **meraa naam** Maria Da Silva **hai.
mãĩ nars hũũ.**

d **meraa naam** Kulwinder Kaur **hai.
mãĩ DaakTar hũũ.**

e **meraa naam** Mohammad Yunus **hai.
mãĩ bas Draaiivar hũũ.**

f **meraa naam** Uma Joshi **hai.
mãĩ vakiil hũũ.**

2
Cross purposes
Match the answers in the second column with the questions or greetings in the first.

a	**assalaam alaikum**	1	Rashida
b	**kyaa haal hai?**	2	Leeds **mẽ**
c	**aapkaa naam kyaa hai?**	3	**vaalaikum assalaam**
d	**aap kahãã rahtii hãĩ?**	4	**Thiik hai**
e	**aur aap kahãã kaam kartii hãĩ?**	5	Headingley Road **par**
f	Leeds **mẽ kahãã?**	6	**mãĩ bas mẽ jaatii hũũ**
g	**aap vahãã kaise jaatii hãĩ?**	7	Bradford **mẽ**

3
Nosy parker
You meet someone for the first time. You want to find out as much about him as possible. What do you say to get the following information?

- a   His name
- b   Where he lives
- c   Where he works
- d   What his job is
- e   How he gets there

4
Here, there and everywhere
Balwinder Singh and Jagdish Malhotra have just met in the centre of Gloucester. Fill in the blanks with **yahãã, vahãã** or **kahãã**.

Balwinder: **aap _____ rahte hãĩ?**
Jagdish: **mãĩ** Bristol **mẽ rahtaa hũũ.**
Balwinder: **aur aap _____ kaam karte hãĩ?**
Jagdish: Gloucester **mẽ.**
Balwinder: Gloucester **mẽ? aap _____ kaise aate hãĩ?**
Jagdish: **bas mẽ.**
Balwinder: **mãĩ bhii _____ kaam kartaa hũũ.**
Jagdish: Gloucester **mẽ _____?**
Balwinder: London Road **par.**
Jagdish: **aur aap _____ rahte hãĩ?**
Balwinder: Stroud **mẽ.**
Jagdish: **aap _____ kaise jaate hãĩ?**
Balwinder: **mãĩ _____ se _____ kaar mẽ jaataa hũũ.**

5
Answering back
Jenny Taylor is a teacher living in Islington. Every day she drives to work in Hackney. How does she answer these questions?

a aap kahãã rahtii hãĩ?
b aap kyaa kaam kartii hãĩ?
c aap kahãã kaam kartii hãĩ?
d aap vahãã kaise jaatii hãĩ?

6
You and I
Choose one of the words in the first column to fit with each of the phrases in the second column.

aap
mãĩ

a bas mẽ jaate hãĩ
b Liverpool mẽ rahtii hũũ
c Leeds mẽ kaam kartaa hũũ
d Tren mẽ aatii hãĩ

7
Men and women
Fill in the gaps with the right -taa form

 8

Listening exercise

Listen to the interviews on the tape. Sneh is asking different people about their jobs, where they work and where they live. Some of this information is given in the table below, but it is incomplete. See if you can fill the gaps.

NAME	JOB	PLACE OF WORK	AREA OF RESIDENCE
Nazir-ul-Haq	teacher	Handsworth College	Yardley
Tejinder Kaur			
Dipak Patel			
Jean MacDonald			

BACKGROUND

HINDI AND URDU IN THE INDIAN SUB-CONTINENT

If you were to travel overland through cities, towns and villages from West Punjab in Pakistan, eastwards through Northern India, all the way down to Calcutta in West Bengal and then on to Dhaka, the capital of Bangladesh, as you moved from one place to the next, you'd find differences in language between neighbouring towns and villages. These differences would be large enough to distinguish local varieties, but not so large that people couldn't understand each other. But, as you kept moving, all these little differences would add together so that by the time you'd reached Uttar Pradesh, the local languages there would be significantly different from that of the place where you started out. And by the time you'd reached your journey's end in Bangladesh, the local languages there would be very different again.

So, across this whole area there is a continuum of *local languages* – languages for use within the local community and inside the home. In some cases one of these languages will have a wider *regional* status. Punjabi, Gujarati and Bengali, for example, are all standardised languages, each with its own script and literary tradition.

In addition to these local and regional languages, there are also *link languages* which have a wider currency – which you are likely to hear in use (with some variation, of course) anywhere in Pakistan and Northern India and occasionally in Bangladesh too. Some people used to call the common spoken language of the market place Hindustani, but that is a rather old-fashioned term these days, and the constitutions of neither India nor Pakistan recognise this name. Hindi, however, is the official national language of India, and Urdu is given the same status in Pakistan. It is also recognised as a major language in India. The history of these languages will be dealt with in the next unit.

Major areas for
settlers to
Britain

PAKISTAN
The North-West Frontier Province
Pathans and others (Muslim)
The Province of Punjab
Punjabis (Muslim)
The Mirpur Border Area with Kashmir
Kashmiris (Muslim)

PAKISTAN

Delhi

INDIA

Karachi

Calcutta

BANGLADESH

BURMA

Bombay

INDIA
Areas of Gujarat
and the Kutch
Gujaratis (Hindu)

The Punjab State
Punjabis (Sikh)

Madras

BANGLADESH
The border with Assam
(India)~ Sylhet
Bengalis (Muslim)

The Maritime
'East Indian' Area
Bengalis (Muslim)

milkar baRii Khushii huii

VISITING SOMEONE'S HOME

TALKING ABOUT YOUR FAMILY

 1

If you visit a friend's house you may be introduced to the family. Here Anita visits Shain's home and first meets some of the senior family members:

Shain:	**ye mere Khaavind h͠aĩ. inkaa naam** Farid **(fariid) hai.**
Anita:	**assalaam alaikum.**
Farid:	**vaalaikum assalaam.**
Shain:	**aur ye mere vaalid h͠aĩ.**
Anita:	**milkar baRii Khushii huii.**
Mr Ramzan:	**bahut meharbaanii.**
Shain:	**aur ye merii vaalidaa h͠aĩ.**
Anita:	**assalaam alaikum.**
Mrs Ramzan:	**vaalaikum assalaam.**

NOTES

When introducing senior family members it is customary to show respect by using **hãĩ** (are) rather than **hai** (is):

ye mere Khaavind* hãĩ   This is my husband
this my   husband   is

Here, to show respect, 'husband' is treated as plural, so a literal translation might be 'These are my husband'.

And in the same way:

aur ye mere vaalid* hãĩ   And this is my father
and this my   father   is

aur ye merii vaalidaa* hãĩ   And this is my mother
and this my   mother   is

For female relatives you use the feminine **merii** instead of masculine (plural) **mere**.

* These are the Urdu words – for Hindi equivalents see *Keywords* on p. 40.

To introduce the name of someone you respect you could say:

inkaa naam Farid **hai.**   His name is Farid
his   name   Farid is

inkaa is a plural form (more literally 'their') which doesn't change for the sex of the person, so you would use **inkaa naam** for 'her name' as well.

Learn **milkar baRii Khushii huii** as a complete phrase, which means 'Pleased to meet you'. You can reply to it by repeating the same thing, or saying **bahut meharbaanii** – 'Thank you very much'.

CHECK-UP 1 Which family members has Anita met so far?

2

Later Anita meets Shain's younger brother and her children too:

Anita: **ye kaun hãĩ?**
Shain: **ye meraa chhoTaa bhaaii hai. iskaa naam** Urfan **(urfaan) hai.
aur ye meraa beTaa hai.**
Anita: **iskaa naam kyaa hai?**
Shain: **iskaa naam** Amar **(amar) hai.**
Anita: **aur aapke kitne bachche hãĩ?**
Shain: **hamaare tiin bachche hãĩ. ek beTaa aur do beTiyãã.**
Anita: **achchhaa, do beTiyãã bhii hãĩ. aur iskaa naam kyaa hai?**
Shain: **iskaa naam** Amra **(aamraa) hai, aur iskaa naam** Aneesha **(aniishaa) hai.**

NOTES

If you want to ask who someone is, you can say:

ye   kaun hãĩ?   Who is this?
this who is

these who are   Who are they?

This question can be ambiguous. It's plural so you might be asking about several individuals, or you could be asking about just one person to whom you are showing respect. You can only tell from the context.

When introducing *junior* family members there is no need to use the plural forms:

ye meraa chhoTaa bhaaii hai This is my younger brother.
this my   small   brother is

ye meraa beTaa hai   This is my son.
this my   son   is

When introducing a junior relative's name you can say:

iskaa naam Urfan **hai.**   His name is Urfan.
his   name Urfan is
iskaa naam Amra **hai.**   Her name is Amra.
her   name Amra   is

iskaa is a *singular* form meaning 'his' *or* 'her'.

Anita also asks Shain how many children they have:

aapke kitne   **bachche hãĩ?** How many children have you
your   how many children are   got?

Here the word for 'your' – **aapke** – has changed, as we've already seen with **meraa, mere,** and **merii,** to agree with the masculine plural **bachche** – 'children'.

Shain tells her:

hamaare tiin   bachche hãĩ.   We have three children.
our   three children are
ek beTaa aur do beTiyãã   One son and two daughters.
one son   and two daughters

CHECK-UP 2 What are the names of Shain's daughters?

3

Mrs Ramzan shows Anita the family album:

Mrs Ramzan: **ye mere baRe bhaaii hãĩ. inkaa naam** Aslam **(aslam) hai.**
Anita: **ye kahãã rahte hãĩ?**
Mrs Ramzan: Birmingham **mẽ.**
Anita: **aur ye kaun hãĩ?**
Mrs Ramzan: **ye merii baRii bahan hãĩ. inkaa naam** Asmat **(asmat) hai.**
Anita: **ye kyaa kaam kartii hãĩ?**
Mrs Ramzan: **ye** social worker **hãĩ.**
Anita: **aap kitne bhaaii-bahanẽ hãĩ?**
Mrs Ramzan: **ham das hãĩ.**

NOTES

Mrs Ramzan points out her elder brother and sister:
ye   mere baRe bhaaii hãĩ   This is my elder brother.
this my   big   brother is
ye   merii baRii bahan hãĩ   This is my elder sister.
this my   big   sister is

Anita asks about them:
ye kahãã rahte hãĩ?   Where does he live?
this where living is
ye kahãã kaam kartii hãĩ?   Where does she work?
this where work   doing is

She asks how many brothers and sisters there are:
aap kitne   bhaaii-bahanẽ hãĩ? How many brothers and
you how many brothers-sisters are   sisters are you?

Notice that when brothers and sisters are gathered together the whole group is considered (at least for grammatical purposes) to be masculine plural.
Mrs Ramzan includes herself in the total:
ham das hãĩ   We are ten.
we   ten are

CHECK-UP 3 What does Mrs Ramzan's elder sister do?

KEYWORDS

△ **ye . . . h̃aı̃** — this is . . . (respectful)
△ **Khaavind** (m) — husband (Urdu)
△ **inkaa** — his/her (respectful)
△ **aur** — and
△ **vaalid** (m) — father (Urdu)
△ **milkar baRii Khushii huii** — pleased to meet you
△ **bahut meharbaanii** — thank you very much
△ **vaalidaa** (f) — mother (Urdu)
△ **pati** (m) — husband (Hindi)
△ **pitaa** (m) — father (Hindi)
△ **maataa** (f) — mother (Hindi)

△ **kaun** — who?
△ **ye . . . hai** — this is . . .
△ **chhoTaa** — small, younger
△ **bhaaii** (m) — brother
△ **iskaa** — his/her
△ **beTaa** (m) — son
△ **kitne** — how many
△ **bachche** (m) — children
△ **hamaare** — our
△ **tiin** — three
△ **ek** — one
△ **do** — two
△ **beTiyãã** (f) — daughters
△ **achchhaa** — I see/Well . . .

△ **baRe/baRii** — big, elder
△ **bahan** (f) — sister
△ **bhaaii-bahanẽ** (m) — brothers and sisters
△ **ham . . . h̃aı̃** — we are . . .
△ **das** — ten

△ **biivii** (f) — wife (Urdu)
△ **patnii** (f) — wife (Hindi)
△ **chaar** — four

SOUND SYSTEMS

b AND bh

The initial sounds at the beginning of the words for 'brother' and 'sister' – **bhaaii** and **bahan** – introduce an important set of sound distinctions in Hindi and Urdu. You'll notice that the **b** at the beginning

of **bahan** is quite similar to the English **b** in 'aboard'. **bh** is quite a different sound, however, with no close English equivalent. You have to pronounce **bh** with a breathy voice. Listen carefully to hear the difference. There is the same difference between **g** and **gh, j** and **jh, D** and **Dh, d** and **dh, R** and **Rh.**

HOW THE LANGUAGE WORKS

ONE OR MORE THAN ONE

The Hindi and Urdu numbers are given on pages 191–2. In English we normally change word endings according to the number of people or things being referred to – 'one sister' (singular), 'two sister*s*' (plural), 'one child' (singular), 'two child*ren*' (plural). A similar thing happens in Hindi and Urdu, though there are different patterns for masculine and feminine.

Masculine nouns can be put into two groups – those that end in **-aa**, and those that don't. Feminine nouns can also be put into groups – those that end in **-ii** and those that don't. The table below shows the general pattern of how the word endings change for each of these groups according to number. You'll see that only masculine nouns not ending in **-aa** don't change. There are of course some exceptions. **pitaa** for example does not change in the plural.

	Singular	Plural
Masculine	**ek beTaa**	**do beTe**
	ek bhaaii	**do bhaaii**
Feminine	**ek beTii**	**do beTiyā̃**
	ek bahan	**do bahanẽ**

BIG AND SMALL

Words which are used to describe something like **baRaa** and **chhoTaa** ('big' and 'small', but when referring to relatives meaning 'older' or 'younger') are *adjectives.* **meraa, aapkaa, iskaa,** etc are also adjectives. Any adjectives ending in **-aa/-ii** have to change according to the number and gender of the things or people they describe. In fact they're not difficult to learn as they take almost exactly the same endings as the **-aa** and **-ii** nouns:–

mer*aa* chhoT*aa* beTaa	masculine singular
my little son	
mer*ii* chhoT*ii* beTii	feminine singular
my little daughter	

mer*e* chhoT*e* beTe	masculine plural
my little sons	

mer*ii* chhoT*ii* beTiyaã	feminine plural
my little daughters	

'THESE ARE MY FATHER'

We have seen that in Hindi and Urdu you treat someone respectfully by referring to him or her as more than one person:–

ye mere vaalid haĩ   'These are my father'

Although verbs and adjectives become *plural* you will see that the noun itself stays *singular*. **aapkii biivii kaisii haĩ?** is a polite way of asking a man about his wife's health. **aapkii biiviyaã kaisii haĩ?** assumes he has more than one wife.

URDU AND HINDI HAVE NO 'HAVE'

There is no direct equivalent of 'have' in Hindi and Urdu. We've seen that for 'we have four children' you would say **hamaare chaar bachche haĩ** (literally 'our four children are') using the possessive adjective **hamaaraa.** If you want to say 'I have four children' say **mere chaar bachche haĩ,** using **mere** ('my') instead of **hamaare.** This is the normal way of referring to possessions that can't be taken away, like relatives, or parts of the body. We shall see in Unit 5 that for other kinds of possessions like money and property, which you might have one day but lose the next, a different structure is used.

EXERCISES

1

Cross purposes

Here's a conversation between two neighbours. Rashida Begum's replies have got mixed up. Can you put them in the right order?

Usha Patel

Rashida Begum

a **aap kitne bhaaii-bahanẽ haĩ?**

b **achchhaa, aur ye kaun haĩ?**

c **iskaa naam kyaa hai?**

d **aur iskaa?**

e **hamaare do beTe haĩ.**

f **ham chaar haĩ. mere ek baRe bhaaii haĩ, aur merii do bahanẽ bhii haĩ.**

1 **ye** Salma **(salmaa) hai.**
  aapke kitne bachche haĩ?

2 **iskaa naam** Safdar **(safdar) hai.**

3 **ye mere bachche haĩ. ek beTaa aur ek beTii.**

4 **achchhaa, aur aap kitne bhaaii-bahanẽ haĩ?**

5 **ham do haĩ. maĩ aur meraa chho Taa bhaaii.**

2
Starting up
Your friend Sukwinder Kaur meets you in a sweet centre with her sister Kulwinder and Kulwinder's daughter Manjit. You start up a conversation with Kulwinder. What do you say?

	You	*Kulwinder*
a	_____	**sat srii akaal.**
b	_____	**Thiik hũũ.**
c	_____	**mãĩ Tiichar hũũ.**
d	_____	Charles St School **mẽ.**
e	_____	**do.** Manjit, **aur ek beTaa bhii hai.**
f	_____	**ham do hãĩ, mãĩ aur merii bahan,** Sukwinder.

3
Family crossword

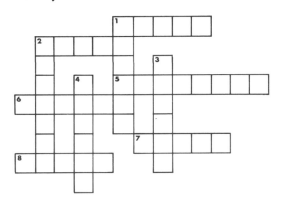

Across
1 sister
2 daughter
5 mother (Urdu)
6 brother
7 father (Hindi)
8 son

Down
1 wife (Urdu)
2 children
3 father (Urdu)
4 mother (Hindi)

4
Odd one out
In each group there is a word that doesn't belong. Which is it?

a **biivii   bas   bahan   beTaa**
b **dukaandaar   DaakTar   vakiil   vaalid**
c **bas   kaar   naam   Tren**

5

My, my, my

The word for 'my' is missing from the following sentences. Choose either **meraa, merii,** or **mere** to fill each gap.

a   ye _____ baRe bhaaii haĩ.

b   ye _____ chhoTii bahan hai.

c   ye _____ beTaa hai.

d   ye _____ biivii haĩ.

e   ye _____ bahanẽ haĩ.

f   _____ do bhaaii haĩ.

g   _____ do beTe haĩ.

h   _____ chaar bahanẽ haĩ.

6

His and hers

Balwant Singh is introducing his family to his friend Frank Brooks. Fill in the blanks following the example. Remember to choose between **inkaa** and **iskaa**.

e.g.

Jatinder

ye merii biivii haĩ. inkaa naam Jatinder hai

Sardul Singh

a   ye mere pitaajii haĩ. _____ _____ _____ _____ _____

Tarsem Kaur

b   ye merii maataajii haĩ. _____ _____ _____ _____ _____

Ranjit

c   ye meraa beTaa hai. _____ _____ _____ _____

Bhupinder

d   ye merii beTii hai. _____ _____ _____ _____

7
Counting up

This family tree shows how many brothers, sisters, sons and daughters you have. Fill in the blanks following the example. Remember to choose the right form of **meraa/mere/merii.**

e.g. **merii ek bahan hãĩ**

a _____ _____ bhaaii hãĩ
b _____ _____ beTii hai
c _____ _____ beTe hãĩ
d _____ _____ bachche hãĩ
e _____ _____ bhaaii-bahanẽ hãĩ
f (or **ham** _____ bhaaii-bahanẽ hãĩ)

8
Listening exercise

Uma Patel is showing her family album to Harbans Kaur. Listen to the tape and see if you can complete her family tree.

BACKGROUND

THE DEVELOPMENT OF MODERN HINDI AND URDU

Modern Hindi and Urdu are of course completely different from their remote ancestor Sanskrit, and records of their development out of this classical language are incomplete. The earliest writings in a language recognised as an immediate ancestor of Hindi and Urdu are those of Amir Khusro (1253–1327), scholar, poet, and musician. Khusro, although Turkish himself, wrote in a language he called Hindavi, the language spoken in and around Delhi, where his family had settled some generations previously.

About this time in the army camps around Delhi many other languages were being spoken as well as Hindavi, including Turkish, Persian and Punjabi. Gradually, more and more words from these languages were absorbed into the surrounding Hindavi grammatical framework. In this way a distinctive camp language developed, which came to be known as Urdu (the Turkish word for 'camp' or 'army').

As time passed and more literature was produced the language names 'Hindavi' (later 'Hindi') and 'Urdu' came to be associated with different scripts and religious communities. Nowadays in some literary and educated styles you will find in Urdu a very heavy influence, especially in vocabulary, of Persian and Arabic, and in Hindi of Sanskrit. However, some writers and speakers prefer to use mostly the words which both Urdu and Hindi *share*, so (apart from the choice of script) it becomes an open question as to whether they are using Urdu *or* Hindi. As an introduction to spoken Urdu *and* Hindi this book concentrates on what the languages have in common.

So you can see how it would be a mistake to associate Urdu exclusively with Muslims and Hindi exclusively with Hindus. The two languages have always developed side by side and exerted great influence on each other. In India and Pakistan you will find Muslims, Hindus, Sikhs, Christians, Buddhists, Jains, Jews and Parsees among those who speak Hindi or Urdu, and many would say they speak *both*.

isko kyaa kahte hãĩ?

ASKING THE NAMES OF THINGS

TALKING ABOUT FOOD

MAKING POLITE REQUESTS

 1

Anita talked to Mrs Raval at a Handsworth sweet centre. She wanted to find out about some of the food on sale:

Anita:	**namaste bahan jii.**
Mrs Raval:	**namaste.**
Anita:	**ye kyaa hai?**
Mrs Raval:	**ye pulaav hai.**
Anita:	**ismẽ kyaa hai?**
Mrs Raval:	**chaaval, sabzii, ghii, aur masaale hãĩ.**
Anita:	**kyaa ismẽ mirch bhii hai?**
Mrs Raval:	**jii nahĩĩ, ismẽ mirch nahĩĩ hai.**
Anita:	**aur ye kyaa hai?**
Mrs Raval:	**raaytaa.**
Anita:	**ismẽ kyaa hai?**
Mrs Raval:	**dahii, aaluu, aur namak.**
Anita:	**kyaa garam masaalaa bhii Daalte hãĩ?**
Mrs Raval:	**jii, Daalte hãĩ.**

NOTES

If you want to ask what something is, you can say:

ye kyaa hai?   What is this?
this what is

The answer is straightforward:

ye pulaav hai   This is pilao.
this pilao   is

You may want to ask what's *in* something:

ismē kyaa hai?   What's in this?
this-in what is

And to ask if there are additional ingredients:

kyaa   ismē mirch bhii hai?
(question) this-in chilli   also is

                Is there chilli in this as well?

kyaa   garam masaalaa bhii Daalte hāĩ?
(question) garam   masala   also putting are

                Do you/they also put garam
                masala in it?

The negative answer is quite simple:

jii   nahīĩ. ismē mirch nahīĩ hai
(respectful) no.   this-in chilli   not   is

                No. There's no chilli in it.

And if the answer is yes:

jii   hāã.   Yes.
(respectful) yes

This is often shortened simply to **jii** – yes. To make it a bit more
emphatic you repeat the verb:

jii,   Daalte hāĩ   Yes, we/they do (put it in).
(respectful) putting are

CHECK-UP 1 What are the ingredients of Mrs Raval's raita?

2

Out shopping Gordon asked Anita what things were called and how
they were used:

Gordon: **ye kyaa hai?**
Anita: **isko dhaniyaa kahte hāĩ.**
Gordon: **achchhaa, isko kyaa karte hāĩ?**
Anita: **isko daal-sabzii mē Daalte hāĩ.**
Gordon: **achchhaa, aur isko kyaa kahte hāĩ?**
Anita: **isko methii kahte hāĩ.**
Gordon: **isko kyaa karte hāĩ?**

Anita:	**isko pakaate h̃aĩ.**
Gordon:	**achchhaa, methii ko angrezii m̃e kyaa kahte h̃aĩ?**
Anita:	**maaluum nah̃ĩ.**
Gordon:	**aur usko kyaa kahte h̃aĩ?**
Anita:	**vo paalak hai. usko angrezii m̃e** 'spinach' **kahte h̃aĩ.**

NOTES

If you want to give the name of something, you can say:

isko   dhaniyaa kahte h̃aĩ   We/they call this 'dhaniya'.
this-to 'dhaniya' saying are

Note the use of the postposition **ko**. In Hindi and Urdu you have to 'call *to* this dhaniya'. (If you need to refresh your memory about postpositions then refer back to Unit 2, p. 26.)

And if you want to ask what something is called, put **kyaa** in place of the name:

isko   kyaa kahte h̃aĩ?   What do you/they call this?
this-to what saying are

To ask how herbs or vegetables are used, say:

isko   kyaa karte h̃aĩ?   What do you/they do with this?
this-to what doing are

To say they are cooked as a main dish (rather than simply added as seasoning):

isko   pakaate h̃aĩ   We/they cook it.
this-to cooking are

You may want to ask what something is called in English:

methii ko angrezii mē kyaa kahte hãĩ?
'methii'-to English-in   what saying are?

                            What is **methii** called in
                            English?

If you want to ask or talk about something that is *distant* rather than *near* use **vo** and **usko** instead of **ye** and **isko**: **vo paalak hai** – *That's* spinach, **usko kyaa kahte hãĩ?** – What's *that* called?

There is a common stock phrase for 'I don't know' – **maaluum nahĩĩ** – literally 'known not'.

CHECK-UP 2 How is coriander used?

3

You may want to ask the waiter some questions next time you go to a restaurant:

Waiter:	**assalaam alaikum.**
Anjum:	**vaalaikum assalaam. meraa naam** Anjum **(anjum) hai.**
Waiter:	**aaiye. ye aapkii mez hai. tashriif rakhiye. aaj kaa** menu **liijiye saahab.**
Anjum:	**shukriyaa . . . ye kyaa hai?**
Waiter:	**ye dhansak hai.**
Anjum:	**dhansak? ismē kyaa Daalte hãĩ?**
Waiter:	**daal, sabzii, gosht, aur mirch-masaale.**
Anjum:	**Thiik hai. dhansak kii ek pleT laaiye.**

NOTES

The waiter welcomes the customer:

aaiye	Please come in.
please-come	
ye aapkii mez hai	This is your table.
this your table is	
tashriif rakhiye*	Please take a seat.
presence please-place	
aaj kaa menu **liijiye saahab**	Here is today's menu.
today-of menu please-take sir	

* Very formal Urdu.

After making some enquiries the customer gives his order:

dhansak kii ek pleT laaiye
dhansak -of one plate please-bring

Can I have dhansak please.

We've already seen how **kaa, ke** and **kii** can be added to **aap** – **aapkaa, aapkii** etc, to mean 'your' (literally 'you-of'). **kaa/ke/kii** may also follow *nouns* (as with **aaj** and **dhansak**) to link them with the following word. Again, (as with **aapkaa**) they agree in gender with the *following* noun. Here 'menu' is masculine and **pleT** is feminine.

CHECK-UP 3 Is dhansak a vegetarian dish?

KEYWORDS

△	**pulaav** (m)	pilao
△	**ism̃ẽ**	in this
△	**chaaval** (m)	rice
△	**sabzii** (f)	vegetable
△	**ghii** (m)	clarified butter/ghee
△	**masaale** (m)	spices
△	**mirch** (f)	chilli
△	**nahĩĩ**	no, not
△	**jii nahĩĩ**	no
△	**raaytaa** (m)	raita
△	**dahii** (m)	yoghurt
△	**aaluu** (m)	potato
△	**namak** (m)	salt
△	**garam masaalaa** (m)	mixed spices
△	**Daal**	put
△	**jii h̃ãã**	yes
△	**jii**	yes

△	**isko**	'to' this
△	**dhaniyaa** (m)	coriander
△	**kah**	call, say
△	**daal** (f)	lentils
△	**methii** (f)	fenugreek
△	**pakaa**	cook
△	**angrezii** (f)	English
△	**maaluum nahīī**	I don't know
△	**usko**	'to' that
△	**vo**	that
△	**paalak** (f)	spinach
△	**aaiye**	please come
△	**mez** (f)	table
△	**tashriif rakhiye**	please sit down (very formal Urdu)
△	**aaj**	today
△	**kaa/ke/kii**	'of' (postposition)
△	**liijiye**	please take
△	**saahab** (m)	sir
△	**shukriyaa***	thank you
△	**gosht** (m)	meat
△	**pleT** (f)	plate
△	**laaiye**	please bring
△	**baiThiye**	please sit down (Hindi and less formal Urdu)
△	**rakh**	place
△	**le**	take
△	**laa**	bring
△	**baiTh**	sit
△	**dhanyavaad****	thank you

* Urdu   ** Hindi

SOUND SYSTEMS

d AND D

The sentence **daal mẽ kyaa Daalte hãĩ?** (What do they put in the lentils?) is a good example of a sound distinction which many English speakers find difficult to hear, at least until they get used to it. **daal** and **Daal** are two *different* words. The problem with the English alphabet is that it doesn't have enough letters to represent all the different sounds of Hindi and Urdu, so this book uses small **d** to represent a different sound from capital **D**. The **D** sound is made by turning the tip of the tongue back so it's actually the underside of it which touches the roof of the mouth. Linguists call this *retroflex*.

T and **R** are also retroflex sounds. The **d** sound in Hindi and Urdu however is dental – it's made with the tongue between the teeth, (in the same position as for the *th* in English 'then'). **t** is also dental in Hindi and Urdu. In English d and t are pronounced with the tongue slightly *behind* the teeth. Such English pronunciations sound more like **D** and **T** than **d** and **t** to speakers of Urdu and Hindi. So remember – bring the tongue well *forward* for **d** and **t** in Hindi and Urdu.

HOW THE LANGUAGE WORKS

MISSING PERSONS
In Unit 1 we saw you can say **Thiik hũũ** for **mãĩ Thiik hũũ**. Words for 'I, you, he, they' etc (subject pronouns) are usually dropped when their meaning is clearly understood from the context. A similar thing happens in English. When someone asks 'How are you?' you may reply 'Fine, thanks'. If someone asks you how you are you don't normally answer by talking about someone else's health.

Sometimes in Hindi and Urdu the subject is omitted from the sentence in order to be *deliberately* indefinite. In the sentence **angrezii mẽ paalak ko** 'spinach' **kahte hãĩ**, *someone* is calling **paalak** spinach, but no one really knows or cares *who*.

WHAT'S WHAT?
The word **kyaa** in Hindi and Urdu has another meaning apart from 'what' (as in **aapkaa naam** *kyaa* **hai?**). It can also be used to introduce straightforward yes/no questions like **kyaa aap** London **mẽ rahte hãĩ?** – 'Do you live in London?' When used in this way it is not stressed and is spoken rather quickly.

THIS AND THAT, AND HIM AND HER
The most basic meaning of **ye** is 'this' or 'these', (though we've seen in Unit 3 it is sometimes more naturally translated into English by he, she, it, or they). We've now seen **ismẽ** for 'in this', as well as **iskaa** ('of this') and **inkaa** ('of these').

ismẽ kyaa hai?	What's in this?
inkaa naam Farid hai	His (respectful) name is Farid
iskaa naam kyaa hai?	What's his/her (informal) name?

ye, when followed by a *postposition* (like **mẽ, ko** or **kaa**) changes to either **is** or **in**. (See Unit 2, p. 26 if you want to remind yourself about postpositions.) **ye** is the 'direct form' and **is/in** the 'oblique form'. The same thing happens with **vo**, which basically means 'that' or 'those' but again sometimes is better translated as he, she, it, or they:

		Direct	Oblique	Example (+**kaa** – 'of')
Near	Singular ('this')	**ye**	**is**	**iskaa** of this
	Plural ('these')	**ye**	**in**	**inkaa** of these
Far	Singular ('that')	**vo**	**us**	**uskaa** of that
	Plural ('those')	**vo**	**un**	**unkaa** of those

These forms are the ones you will come across most often in every-day speech, but you will find slightly different *direct* forms in written and *carefully spoken* Hindi:

yah	This	**vah**	That
ye	These	**ve**	Those

We'll be coming across 'direct' and 'oblique' forms again in later units, so it's worth remembering these names. There's no exact equivalent in English but it's a bit like the difference between 'he' and 'him', or 'she' and 'her'. 'He gave it to she' is bad English – you can't have 'she' (or 'he') after a preposition like 'to' in English anymore than you can have **ye** or **vo** before a postposition like **ko** in Hindi and Urdu.

BEING NEGATIVE

nahĩĩ is both 'not' and 'no', though a properly polite 'no' should be preceded by **jii** – **jii nahĩĩ**. In negative sentences the word for is/am/are is often omitted. Both the following sentences are correct and mean the same thing:

ismē mirch nahĩĩ　　　　There's no chilli in it.
ismē mirch nahĩĩ hai

In a sentence with a **-taa** form verb the **nahĩĩ** will usually come directly before the **-taa** form and **hãĩ/hai/hũũ** is *usually* omitted:

mãĩ Dudley **mē nahĩĩ rahtaa**　　I don't live in Dudley.
I　Dudley-in　not　living

SAY PLEASE

It is possible to make a direct translation of the word 'please' into Hindi and Urdu, but the normal way of making a polite request is to add **-iye** to the verb stem:

Stem	'+please'	
aa	**aaiye**	please come
rakh	**rakhiye**	please place
le	**liijiye***	please take
laa	**laaiye**	please bring
baiTh	**baiThiye**	please sit

* Other irregular forms are listed in the Grammatical Summary.

EXERCISES

1
Mixed vegetables

This conversation over a sweet centre counter has got rather muddled. Can you put it in order? (At sweet centres you can also buy savouries.)

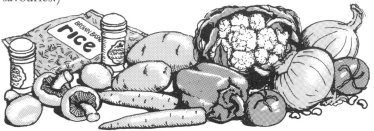

	Customer		Waiter
a	**ye kyaa hai?**	1	'vegetable'.
b	**shukriyaa**	2	**jii hāā, sabzii**
c	**sabzii?**	3	**namaste jii**
d	**namaste**	4	**liijiye jii.**
e	**sabzii ko angrezii mē kyaa kahte hāī?**	5	**chaaval, sabzii, ghii, aur masaale.**
f	**Thiik hai, iskii ek pleT laaiye.**	6	**ye pulaav hai.**
g	**ismē kyaa Daalte hāī?**		

2
Dinner time

You visit a friend's house for a meal. You don't know much about South Asian food and cookery but you'd like to find out.

a Before eating she takes you into the back garden where she grows some herbs and vegetables. She shows you a plant you don't recognise. How do you ask what it is?

b She tells you the name, **methii**, but you don't know the word. How do you ask what **methii** is in English?

c She tells you it's called fenugreek in English (which may or may not leave you any the wiser). So how do you ask her how it's used in cooking?

d Afterwards you sit down to dinner. You're given a dish you don't recognise. How do you ask what it's called?

e You'd like to know what the ingredients are. How do you ask what's in it?

f You want to check it's a vegetarian dish. How do you ask if there's any meat in it?

3
What's in it?

a ye raaytaa hai. ismẽ kyaa Daalte hãĩ?

ismẽ  aur Daalte hãĩ.

b  ye pulaav hai. ismẽ kyaa Daalte hãĩ?

ismẽ aur Daalte hãĩ.

c ye dhansak hai. ismẽ kyaa Daalte hãĩ?

ismẽ  aur Daalte hãĩ.

4
Word search
Find twelve words to do with food in this square:

```
k a m a n a r g
a d a l a c i h
l a s d a h i i
a a a r t a h i
a l a l y a t z
p u l a a v e b
r u a m a a m a
a h a z r l T s
```

5
Near and far
Choose the right form of **ye** or **vo** to fill the blanks.

6
Questions, questions

The following words all begin with **k:– kyaa, kahãã, kaise, kaisii, kitne, kitnii.** Fill the blanks in the following questions with one of these words.

a   _____ haal hai?   **Thiik hai**
b   aapkaa naam _____ hai?   ' John Taylor
c   aap _____ rahte hãĩ?   Cardiff **mẽ**
d   aap _____ kaam karte hãĩ?   **mãi** journalist **hũũ**
e   _____ aap Cardiff mẽ kaam   **jii nahĩĩ**
    bhii karte hãĩ?
f   aap _____ kaam karte hãĩ?   Newport **mẽ**
g   aap vahãã _____ jaate hãĩ?   **kaar mẽ**
h   aapkii biivii _____ hãĩ?   Thiik hãĩ, shukriyaa
i   aapke _____ beTe hãĩ?   do
j   aapkii _____ beTiyãã hãĩ?   tiin

7
Yes and no

Choose **hãã** or **nahĩĩ** to fill the gaps.

a   kyaa dhansak mẽ dahii Daalte   jii _____, nahĩĩ Daalte
    hãĩ?
b   kyaa angrezii mẽ methii ko   jii _____, methii ko
    'spinach' **kahte hãĩ?**   'fenugreek' **kahte hãĩ**
c   kyaa methii ko pakaate hãĩ?   jii _____, pakaate hãĩ
d   kyaa daal mẽ namak hai?   jii _____, hai
e   kyaa aapkii bahan London mẽ   jii _____, London mẽ nahĩĩ
    rahtii hãĩ?   rahtii
f   kyaa aap yahãã Tren mẽ aatii   jii _____, bas mẽ aatii hũũ
    hãĩ?
g   kyaa aap Tiichar hãĩ?   jii _____, Tiichar hũũ
h   kyaa aap vakiil hãĩ?   jii _____, mãi Tiichar hũũ
i   kyaa aap DaakTar hãĩ?   jii _____, All Saints Hospital
                                      mẽ kaam kartii hũũ
j   kyaa ismẽ gosht hai?   jii _____, ismẽ gosht nahĩĩ

8
Listening exercise

Listen to three conversations about different dishes. Draw up a table like the one on the next page and, as you listen, tick off the ingredients of each dish.

	1	2	3
chaaval			
namak			
sabzii			
gosht			
mirch			
mirch-masaale			
dahii			
garam masaalaa			
aaluu			

BACKGROUND

URDU AND HINDI IN BRITAIN

The history of Urdu and Hindi in Britain probably goes back as far as the history of contact between Britain and India. Certainly there were Lascars (Indian seamen) living in Britain in the eighteenth century, many of whom would have had a knowledge of these languages. In the post-war era there has been a spectacular rise in numbers of speakers of Hindi and Urdu with the settlement in Britain of Punjabis, Kashmiris, Gujaratis, Bengalis, Pathans and others from the South Asian subcontinent.

South Asian communities in Britain of course speak a wide range of languages, reflecting the different areas from which they've come. They include Gujarati, Bengali, Sylheti, Pushtu, Mirpuri Pahari and Punjabi, with Punjabi probably being the most widely spoken of these. British-born children are often bilingual in English and whichever of these languages is used in the home. Hindi or Urdu are actually the *first language* of comparatively few people who have settled in Britain, and so are not widely used by British-born Asians.

However, in line with the growth in mother tongue teaching in community-based supplementary schools, and to a lesser extent in mainstream education, some Asian children are learning to read and write Urdu or Hindi, either in addition to or instead of, the language of their own homes. Urdu, in particular, is widely taught in Muslim communities around the country.

So, although many people have Hindi or Urdu as a *second* language, don't assume that every South Asian in Britain understands it, far less speaks it. That Hindi and Urdu are as widely understood as they are by British-born Asians is partly due to the popularity of Hindi and

Urdu films, and especially the songs, amongst the younger genera-
tion as much as the older. In later units we take a closer look at the
film industry, as well as at newspapers and other forms of literary and
cultural activity carried out through the medium of Hindi or Urdu.

Asian children learning Hindi and Urdu.

aapko kyaa chaahiye?

SAYING WHAT YOU WANT

ASKING HOW MUCH THINGS ARE

DESCRIBING WHERE THINGS ARE

 1

Omar has just realised he's run out of Basmati rice so he goes out to the corner shop to buy some more:

Omar:	**assalaam alaikum.**
Shopkeeper:	**vaalaikum assalaam. aapkaa kyaa haal hai?**
Omar:	**Thiik hai. aap kaisii hãĩ?**
Shopkeeper:	**mãĩ bhii Thiik hũũ. aapko kyaa chaahiye?**
Omar:	**kyaa aapke paas baasmatii chaaval hãĩ?**
Shopkeeper:	**jii hãã.**
Omar:	**inkii Kiimat kyaa hai?**
Shopkeeper:	**chaaliis pence ke ek paaunD. aapko kitne chaahiyẽ?**
Omar:	**chaar paaunD.**
Shopkeeper:	**liijiye. chaar paaunD.**
Omar:	**shukriyaa.**

NOTES

The shopkeeper asks what Omar wants:

aapko kyaa chaahiye?   What would you like?
you-to what is desirable/required

Omar asks if they have Basmati rice:

kyaa aapke paas baasmatii chaaval hãĩ?
(Q)   you-of near Basmati   rice(pl)   are

Have you got Basmati rice?

He asks the price:

inkii   Kiimat kyaa hai?   How much is it?
these-of price   what is

Remember 'rice' is plural, which is why **inkii** is used. To ask the price of a single item use **iskii** instead of **inkii**. Remember also the use of **kyaa** to introduce yes/no questions.

The shopkeeper tells him:

chaaliis pence **ke ek   paaunD**   Forty pence a pound
forty   pence of one pound

She asks how much he wants:

aapko kitne   chaahiyẽ?   How much do you want?
you-to how many are desirable/required

kitne and **chaahiyẽ** are used because rice is plural. For a singular item use **kitnaa** (masculine) or **kitnii** (feminine) with **chaahiye**.

CHECK-UP 1 How much rice did Omar want?

2

In the event Omar still didn't have enough rice. He went back to get some more, and some coriander as well:

Shopkeeper:	**aapko kyaa chaahiye?**
Omar:	**baasmatii chaaval.**
Shopkeeper:	(to son) **beTe, inko baasmati chaaval chaahiyē.**
Son:	**kahā͠a hā͠i?**
Shopkeeper:	**is** shelf **ke niiche hā͠i. yahā͠a se laaiye.** (to Omar) **aapko aur kyaa chaahiye?**
Omar:	**dhaniyaa.**
Shopkeeper:	**dhaniyaa baahar hai, dukaan ke saamne.**

NOTES

The shopkeeper tells her son what Omar wants:

beTe, inko baasmatii chaaval chaahiyē.

son these-to Basmati rice are desirable/required

Son, this gentleman wants Basmati rice.

beTaa becomes **beTe** because she is addressing her son directly.

The son asks where it is (**kahā͠a hā͠i?**), and the shopkeeper tells him:

is shelf **ke niiche hā͠i.**   It's under this shelf.

this shelf-of below are

She asks Omar what else he wants:

aapko aur kyaa chaahiye?   What else would you like?

you-to more what is desirable/required

Omar wants coriander, so she tells him where it is:

dhaniyaa baahar hai   The coriander is outside.

coriander outside is

dukaan ke saamne   In front of the shop.

shop -of front

Note the use of the English word 'shelf' in an otherwise Hindi or Urdu sentence. As you listen to more and more Hindi and Urdu you are bound to notice how much English is mixed in with them in ordinary conversation. Some people feel the purity of the languages is under threat from English, and where there is a perfectly good Hindi or Urdu word you should make the effort to learn it. But don't be too worried about using English words when you can't think of the proper Hindi or Urdu one. The important thing is to get your message across, and generally people will be more tolerant if a learner uses bad style than if a fluent speaker does.

CHECK-UP 2 Where is the rice?

3

Kamar Shakeel wants to install central heating. The plumber comes round to find out where he wants the radiators:

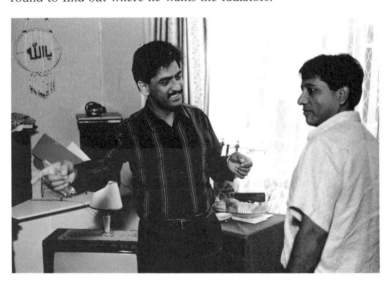

Plumber:	aapke ghar mẽ kitne kamre hãĩ?
Kamar:	aaTh. chaar uupar, aur chaar yahãã niiche.
Plumber:	achchhaa, kyaa radiators khiRkiyõ ke niiche chaahiyẽ?
Kamar:	is chhoTe kamre mẽ mujhe ek hii radiator khiRkii ke niiche chaahiye.
Plumber:	jii, Thiik hai.
Kamar:	aur uupar baRe kamre mẽ ek radiator khiRkii ke niiche chaahiye, aur ek saamne.
Plumber:	Thiik hai.

NOTES

The plumber asks Kamar how many rooms he has:

aapke ghar mẽ kitne kamre hãĩ?
your   house-in how many rooms are

How many rooms are there
in your house?

Kamar tells him:

aaTh. chaar uupar, aur chaar yahãã niiche.
eight four above and four here below

Eight. Four up and four down.

The plumber asks where he wants the radiators:
kyaa radiators **khiRkiyõ ke niiche chaahiyẽ?**
(Q)   radiators windows -of   below   are desirable/required
>   Do you want the radiators
>   under the windows?

First Kamar tells him what he wants 'in this small room' – **is chhoTe kamre mẽ:**
mujhe ek   hii   radiator **khiRkiyõ ke niiche chaahiye**
to me   one only   radiator windows -of   below   is desirable/
required   I want just one radiator below
>   the windows.

Then he tells him what he wants 'up in the big room' – **uupar baRe kamre mẽ:**
ek   radiator **khiRkii ke niiche chaahiye . . .**
one radiator   window -of   below   is desirable
>   I want one radiator below the
>   window.

. . . aur ek   saamne   . . . and one opposite.
and   one front
So **ke saamne** can mean 'opposite' as well as 'in front of'.

CHECK-UP 3 How many radiators does Kamar want in the big room?

KEYWORDS

△	**chaahiye**	is desirable/required
△	**aapko . . . chaahiye**	you want
△	**paas**	near
△	**aapke paas . . . hai**	you have got . . .
△	**baasmatii**	Basmati rice
△	**Kiimat** (f)	price
△	**chaaliis**	forty
△	**paaunD** (m)	pound (weight and money)
△	**chaahiyẽ**	are desirable/required
△	**niiche**	below
△	**is . . . ke niiche**	below this . . .
△	**aur**	more, else
△	**baahar**	outside
△	**saamne**	front
△	**. . . ke saamne**	in front of . . ., opposite

△	**kamre** (m)	rooms
△	**aaTh**	eight
△	**uupar**	above
△	**khiRkii** (f)	window
△	**khiRkiyõ ke niiche**	below the windows
△	**khiRkii ke niiche**	below the window
△	**is . . . kamre mẽ**	in this . . . room
△	**mujhe**	to me
△	**mujhe . . . chaahiye**	I want . . .
△	**kursii** (f)	chair
△	**pakoRaa** (m)	pakora
△	**chaTnii** (f)	chutney

SOUND SYSTEMS

k AND kh

kamraa (room) and **khiRkii** (window) begin with *different* sounds. The **kh** of **khiRkii** is quite similar to the **k** at the beginning of the English word 'kitten', pronounced with a sharp burst of air or 'aspiration'. The **k** of **kamraa**, however, is 'unaspirated', a sound we don't have at the beginnings of words in English. You may find it difficult to hear or produce the difference between **k** and **kh** until you've had some practice. Listen to the difference between the c sounds in 'calf' and 'scarf'. In 'calf' it is *aspirated*, like Hindi and Urdu **kh**, whereas in 'scarf' it is *unaspirated* like Hindi and Urdu **k**. There is the same difference between **ch** and **chh**, **T** and **Th**, **t** and **th**, and **p** and **ph**.

HOW THE LANGUAGE WORKS

OBJECT OF DESIRE

We have translated **aapko kyaa chaahiye** as 'What do you want?', though a more literal translation would be 'What is desirable to you?', or 'What is desired by you?' This indirect way of asking the question is frequently used because in Hindi and Urdu (and other South Asian languages) the desired object is more often the focus of attention than the person desiring it. Note the special form **mujhe** – 'to me'. A complete list of the special forms for 'to you', 'to us' etc. is given in the grammatical summary.

DIRECT AND OBLIQUE

As with the different forms of **ye** and **vo**, which we saw in the previous unit, nouns and adjectives may also change form depending on whether or not they're followed by a postposition. If they *are* fol-

lowed by a postposition they take the oblique form. If not, they take the direct form. For example, the *direct* plural of **khiRkii** ('window') is **khiRkiyãã** ('windows') – like **beTii** and **beTiyãã**, which we saw in Unit 3. But if you want to say '*below* the windows' using the postposition **ke niiche**, then **khiRkiyãã** has to change into its *oblique* form **khiRkiyõ** – **khiRkiyõ ke niiche**.

A full list of the different direct and oblique forms is given in the grammatical summary at the end of the book. If it looks daunting at first, don't worry too much – you'll soon see that the rules are quite regular and that many words don't change much at all.

kamraa (room) is another word that you've learnt in this unit that *does* change. To say '*in* the room', using the postposition **mẽ**, **kamraa** has to change to **kamre** – **kamre mẽ**, 'in the room'. Here **kamre** is the singular oblique form because of the following postposition **mẽ**. Don't be confused by the fact that the plural direct form is also **kamre** – **aapke kitne kamre hãĩ?** 'How many rooms do you have?'. You can always tell if it's singular oblique or plural direct by whether or not it's followed by a postposition. Remember, if it's followed by a postposition it should be oblique.

DIFFERENT POSITIONS
Postpositions in Hindi and Urdu may consist of just one word, like **mẽ**, **par**, and **se**, or more than one, like the new ones we've learnt in this unit:

kursii ke niiche	under the chair
chair -of down	
mez ke saamne	in front of the table
table-of front	

Think of how English has single-word prepositions like 'on' and 'in' and also phrases like 'in front of' or 'on top of' in which a location word is combined with 'of'. Similarly in Hindi and Urdu **ke** can combine with a number of location words (like **saamne**, **niiche** and others) to describe different positions. You will find a list of the most common of these in the grammatical summary at the end of the book.

ke is an oblique form of **kaa**, so remember that when you're combining these phrases with pronouns like **mãĩ** or **ham** or **aap** you need to use the oblique form of **meraa** or **hamaaraa** etc.

mere saamne	in front of me
hamaare saamne	in front of us
aapke saamne	in front of you

kyaa aapke paas chaaval hãĩ? – IS THERE RICE NEAR YOU?

We already know that Hindi and Urdu have no exact equivalent of English 'have' to show *possession*: for example **mere tiin bhaaii hãĩ** literally means 'my three brothers are'. But if the things you possess are *transferable* you express it differently, using **ke paas**, another new postposition:

aapke paas kaar hai   You have a car
your   near car   is

PENCE PER POUND

The formula for 'X pence per pound' is **X** pence **kaa/ke/kii ek paaunD**. Notice that **kaa/ke/kii** does *not* agree with **paaunD** in number and gender, but with *the items whose price is being quoted*. So for rice (masculine plural) say **X** pence *ke* **ek paaunD**, but for sugar (**chiinii** – feminine) say **X** pence *kii* **ek paaunD**.

EXERCISES

1

Cross purposes

The shopkeeper and her customer are at cross-purposes. See if you can put what the customer says in the right order.

Customer

a **inkii Kiimat kyaa hai?**
b **pã̃ ch paaunD. kyaa aapke paas paalak hai?**
c **sat srii akaal**
d **aaj mujhe sabziyãã chaahiyẽ. kyaa aapke paas aaluu hãĩ?**
e **achchhaa, mujhe methii bhii chaahiye**

Shopkeeper

1 **sat srii akaal jii. aapko kyaa chaahiye?**
2 **jii hãã, hãĩ.**
3 **biis pence ke ek paaunD. aapko kitne chaahiyẽ?**
4 **jii hãã, hai**
5 **methii? aaj hamaare paas methii nahĩĩ hai. ye liijiye, aaluu aur paalak.**

2

At the sweet centre

You take a friend to a sweet centre for a snack. It's your treat.

a It's your friend's first visit to a sweet centre. How do you ask him what he would like?
b He points at a trayful of small fried snacks on the counter. He doesn't know what they are. You're not sure either. How do you ask the waiter what they're called?

c The waiter tells you they are pakoras (**pakoRe**). How do you ask him how much they are?

d He tells you they're a pound per pound, or 50p for a plate. How do you tell him you want one plate?

e You sit down at a table waiting for your order and you remember you forgot to ask for chutney (**chaTnii**). How do you ask the waiter if he's got chutney?

f He says he has. How do you ask him to bring a plate of chutney?

3
How much is it?
Here are some things for sale. Fill in the blanks in the questions and answers. You'll find a list of numbers on pages 191–2.

kursii kii Kiimat kyaa hai?   **biis paaunD**

a _____ **kii Kiimat kyaa hai?**   _____ pence **kaa paaunD**

b _____ **kii Kiimat kyaa hai?**   _____ _____ **paaunD**

c _____ **kii Kiimat kyaa hai?**   _____ _____ **paaunD**

d _____ **kii Kiimat kyaa hai?**   _____ _____ **paaunD**

4
What have you got?

This woman is talking about what she's got (and also what she hasn't got). Fill in the blanks with **meraa, mere, merii,** or **mere paas.**

a _____ chaaval kaa ek packet hai

b _____ aaluu nahĩĩ hãĩ

c _____ gosht bhii nahĩĩ hai

d _____ do bachche hãĩ

e _____ ek beTaa hai

f _____ ek beTii bhii hai

g _____ ek hii paaunD hai

5
What do you want?

Translate the following sentences, using the model given. Remember Hindi and Urdu don't normally have equivalents of 'a', 'the', and 'some'. Remember to choose between **chaahiye** and **chaahiyē** depending on whether what you want is singular or plural.

I want some spinach   **mujhe paalak chaahiye**

a I want some rice _____

b I want some coriander _____

c I want some potatoes _____

d I want a house _____

e I want four rooms _____

f I want a car _____

g I want a doctor _____

6
Positions

Choose from **mẽ, par, se, kaa/ke/kii, ke saamne, ke niiche, ke paas,** to fill the gaps in the passage describing the picture below.

kamre _____ ek hii khiRkii hai. khiRkii _____ _____ radiator **hai**. khiRkii _____ _____ mez hai. mez _____ dhansak _____ ek pleT hai. dhansak _____ _____ pulaav _____ pleT bhii hai. mez _____ _____ ek kursii hai. kursii _____ _____ ek bachchaa hai. bachche _____ _____ kaar hai.

7
Endings

Here's a description of someone's house. You'll see some of the word endings are missing. Can you supply them, remembering to choose between *direct* and *oblique* forms?

ye mer_____ ghar hai. mer_____ ghar mẽ chaar kamr_____ hãĩ. tiin choT_____ kamr_____ uupar hãĩ, aur niiche ek hii baR_____ kamr_____ hai. is baR_____ kamr_____ mẽ tiin khiRki_____ hãĩ. ek khiRkii ke niiche ek radiator hai.

 8

Listening exercise – picture dictation

Listen to this conversation in Rama's shop. See if you can spot the mistakes in the picture as Sandra asks where things are.

BACKGROUND

FILM AND VIDEO

It is well known that the Indian film industry is one of the largest in the world, with Bombay having long outstripped Hollywood in terms of numbers of films produced. It is perhaps less well known that Pakistan also produces large numbers of feature films. A large proportion of the films produced in both countries are in Hindi or Urdu.

Films, particularly in India, are a major medium of mass popular entertainment. Big stars of the Indian screen, such as Raj Kapoor, Meena Kumari, and in more recent times Amitabh Bachchan or Rekha, are household names throughout most of the subcontinent. Their private and public lives are subject to minute inspection in the numerous magazines in Hindi, Urdu, English and other languages, which are devoted entirely to the film industry.

Until the end of the 1970s there were many cinemas in Britain which showed exclusively Hindi and Urdu films. However these have now closed as more and more films have become available on video. In most urban centres in Britain you can now find video clubs where you can hire Hindi and Urdu films for a small fee. These may or may not be subtitled in English. Don't get downhearted if the first time you watch one you don't understand a great deal. You're still a beginner at this stage, and if you don't catch something the first time round you can always rewind and play it again.

It's also rather early to be thinking about specialising in either Urdu or Hindi vocabulary, but it's worth noting that there are a number of acknowledged popular classics, such as *Pakeeza* or *Mughal-e-azam*, which, because of the heavy use of Persian and Arabic loanwords, are clearly marked as films in the 'pure' Urdu style. Heavily Sanskritised Hindi films are less common, though you might like to try the lightly Sanskritised popular Indian TV series *Ramayana*, also available on video in Britain, to get a taste of 'pure' Hindi. Most of the lighter popular classics however, such as *Shri 420* or the more recent *Sholay* for example, are in a more neutral style, showing neither a heavy Perso-Arabic nor Sanskrit influence.

Filming at the Red Fort in Agra, India.

Review I

You've now done five out of the ten units in the course, and covered some basic topics and sentence patterns which you can use in a range of social situations – meeting friends or strangers at home, at work, or out in the street, talking about family and food, and going to the shop, sweet centre, or restaurant. Before moving up a gear and launching into the second half of the course, which deals unit by unit with more specialised topics like health, education, or travel, now is a good time to stop and think about what you've learnt so far.

The purpose of this review section is to help you do that and perhaps pinpoint for yourself one or two areas of weakness which you feel you'd like to 'shore up'. It contains a checklist of things you should be able to handle now after Units 1–5 and a series of extra listening exercises for you to choose from if there are any areas where you feel less confident and in which you would like more practice.

CHECKLIST

WHAT CAN I DO, AND WHAT CAN I DO ABOUT IT?

Ask yourself the questions on this questionnaire and tick off the 'yes' or 'no' boxes. If the answer is 'yes' to every one, you're ready for the next stage. If you've answered 'no' to some of the questions then have another look back at the suggested units and try the recommended extra listening exercises.

1   Do I know the different ways of saying hello and goodbye, and asking how someone is?

Yes □ →	Next question
No □ →	Check Unit 1
	Try Exercise A

2	Do I know how to ask someone's name and tell them mine?	Yes □→	Next question
		No □→	Check Unit 1 Try Exercise A
3	Do I know how to find out where someone lives and what their job is, and tell them the same things about myself?	Yes □→	Next question
		No □→	Check Unit 2 Try Exercise B
4	Do I know how to find out where someone works and how they get there, and tell them the same things about myself?	Yes □→	Next question
		No □→	Check Unit 2 Try Exercise B
5	Do I know how to introduce members of my family to a friend?	Yes □→	Next question
		No □→	Check Unit 3 Try Exercise C
6	Do I know how to say how many brothers/sisters/sons/daughters I have and ask someone the same question?	Yes □→	Next question
		No □→	Check Unit 3 Try Exercise D
7	Do I know how to tell a friend about my family – where they live and work and what they do – and ask the friend the same questions?	Yes □→	Next question
		No □→	Check Unit 3 Try Exercise E
8	Do I know how to ask the names of foods and what the ingredients are, and answer the same questions?	Yes □→	Next question
		No □→	Check Unit 4 Try Exercise F, G, H
9	Do I know how to ask what something is called in another language (English, Hindi, or Urdu) and answer the same question?	Yes □→	Next question
		No □→	Check Unit 4 Try Exercise G
10	Do I know how to ask how something is used in cooking?	Yes □→	Next question
		No □→	Check Unit 4 Try Exercise G

| 11 | Do I know how to order food in a restaurant or sweet centre? | Yes ☐ → | Next question |
| | | No ☐ → | Check Unit 4 Try Exercise H |

| 12 | Do I know how to say what, or how much of something, I want (e.g. in a shop)? | Yes ☐ → | Next question |
| | | No ☐ → | Check Unit 5 Try Exercise F, H, I |

| 13 | Do I know how to find out if a shopkeeper has got what I'm looking for, and what the price is? | Yes ☐ → | Next question |
| | | No ☐ → | Check Unit 5 Try Exercise I |

| 14 | Do I know how to ask or explain where something is? | Yes ☐ → | Next unit! |
| | | No ☐ → | Check Unit 5 Try Exercise J |

EXTRA LISTENING EXERCISES

TAKE YOUR PICK

These extra listening exercises deal with some common situations you might find yourself in as a learner. Don't feel you have to go through them all (unless you want to!) but you might like to try some of them, depending on how you got on with the Checklist. Some of them cover more than one question on the Checklist, and for some of the Checklist questions you'll have to do more than just one exercise! Some of the exercises also introduce new words, but it's not necessary to learn them to go on to the rest of the course.

A   Saying hello and saying who you are

Listen to these two conversations between people exchanging names and polite greetings. Don't worry too much about the English spellings of the names if they're unfamiliar to you, but see if you can write down the following information about the speakers. Notice that one of them is *not* feeling well today (**aaj maĩ Thiik nahĩĩ hũũ**). Which one?

1 Names: X. . . . .   *2* Names: P. . . . .
             Y. . . . .   Q. . . . .

Religion . . . .   Religion . . . .

Health: X. . . . .   Health: P. . . . .
          Y. . . . .   Q. . . . .

 B   Talking about yourself

Jaswant Singh and Robert Coleman have just met at a party in Oxford. They talk about their work and where they live. Listen to their conversation and note down as much information as you can about each man.

 C   Introducing a friend to your family

Parvez Khan invites his colleague Martin Cater round for a meal, and introduces him to some of the family. (His mother is visiting Pakistan at the moment.) These are the male members of the family: Amjad, Asif, Shafaq, and Yusuf. How are they related to Parvez? (You'll have to find his father by process of elimination, as he doesn't introduce him by name.) The female family members that Martin meets are Parveen and Nasreen. How are they related to Parvez?

Amjad   . . . .   Nasreen   . . . .
Asif   . . . .   Parveen   . . . .
Shafaq   . . . .
Yusuf   . . . .

 D   Giving personal and family details

Devendra Jain has some financial and family problems on which he needs some advice. He goes to his local advice centre where Baljit Kaur takes down some details. How does she fill in this form?

1   Name: . . . .
2   Address: . . . .
3   Occupation: . . . .
4   Number of children: . . . .
5   Names: . . . .
    . . . .
    . . . .
    . . . .

 E   Getting to know a new friend

Usha and Tarsem are new neighbours. Listen to them talking about themselves and their families and note down as much information about them as you can.

F   Preparing a shopping list

Christine is finding out the ingredients of a special vegetable (**sabzii**) dish that Manju wants to prepare. Some of the ingredients Manju already has, but others Christine will have to go out and buy for her. **pyaaz** (onion), **lahsun** (garlic), **TamaaTar** (tomato), and **gaajar**

(carrot) are among the ingredients, but that's not all . . . Draw up Christine's shopping list.

G   Asking the names of things and their uses

Back in the kitchen again Manju and Christine are asking each other the names of things in the different languages. What are **sarsõ, muulii,** and **pudiinaa?** (Don't look them up in the back of the book!) And what do you do with **muulii?**

H   Ordering food in a restaurant

Ranjit is taking his friends Jerry, Kamaljit, and Sandra out to his favourite restaurant for a meal. Here's the menu. What do they order?

 I   Asking for things at the shop

You're doing a bit of market research into food prices and how much the public is spending in local shops for a consumers' organisation. Listen to this conversation between a shopkeeper and a customer. If you were to interview the customer how would she answer these survey questions? (Don't worry, you can conduct the interview in English!) Remember that numbers are listed in the word lists at the back of the book.

a   What did you buy in the last shop you visited?
b   What were the prices of the items you bought?
c   How much money did you spend there in total?

 J   Finding your way round the shop

There's a new customer in the shop, not yet fluent in Hindi and Urdu, and whose eyesight isn't too good either. Listen to his conversation with the shopkeeper, who patiently explains where the things he's looking for are (spinach, fenugreek, mint, mustard, and radish – check Exercise G if you can't remember what some of these are in Hindi and Urdu). They are standing at the till at the front of the shop, facing each other. Draw a *rough* sketch to show where the different things are. There may be more than one answer. You'll hear some new words for describing positions: **dukaan ke baahar** means 'outside the shop' and **dukaan ke andar** is the opposite – 'inside the shop'. **ke piichhe** means 'behind' so **aapke piichhe** is 'behind you' and **mere piichhe** is 'behind me'. You'll also hear **ke biich mẽ** which means 'between', and **ke uupar**, which means 'above'.

kyaa baat hai?

TALKING ABOUT YOUR HEALTH

DESCRIBING SYMPTOMS

SAYING WHAT YOU'VE DONE

1

Dr Shah is asking his patients about their symptoms:

Naveed:	Hello **DaakTar saahab.**
Dr Shah:	Hello **jii, aap kaise hãĩ?**
Naveed:	**mãĩ Thiik nahĩĩ hũũ.**
Dr Shah:	**kyaa baat hai?**
Naveed:	**mere peT mẽ dard hai.**
Dr Shah:	**kyaa baat hai?**
Waseem:	**thoRaa saa buKhaar hai.**

Dr Shah:	**kyaa baat hai?**
Naheed:	**mujhe sar-dard hai.**

Dr Shah:	**kyaa baat hai?**
Mrs Aggarwal:	**meraa galaa Kharaab hai.**
Dr Shah:	**aapko khãasii bhii hai?**
Mrs Aggarwal:	**jii nahĩ. kal mujhe thoRii sii khãasii thii, magar aaj nahĩ hai.**

NOTES

Dr Shah asks his patients what's wrong:

kyaa baat hai?   What's the matter?
what matter is

They describe their symptoms:

mere peT mẽ dard hai   I have a stomach ache.
my stomach-in pain is
(mujhe) thoRaa saa buKhaar hai
to me little-ish temperature is
                      I have a slight temperature
mujhe sar-dard hai   I have a headache.
to me head pain is
meraa galaa Kharaab hai   I have a sore throat.
my throat bad is

Dr Shah also asks Mrs Aggarwal about other symptoms:

kyaa aapko khãasii bhii hai?   Do you have a cough as well?
(Q) you-to cough also is

Mrs Aggarwal tells him:

kal mujhe thoRii sii khãasii thii . . .
yesterday to me little-ish cough was
                      Yesterday I had a slight
                      cough . . .
. . . magar aaj nahĩ hai   . . . but today I don't.
but today not is

CHECK-UP 1 Who has a slight temperature?

 # 2

Dr Shah also asked Waseem if he had any other problems:

Dr Shah:	**kyaa aapko koii aur taKliif bhii hai?**
Waseem:	**jii hãa. mujhe khãasii bhii hai.**
Dr Shah:	**kal aap baahar gae?**
Waseem:	**jii, mãi dost ke saath shaadii mẽ gayaa.**
Dr Shah:	**aapko sardii lagii hai.**

NOTES

He asks if there are any additional symptoms:

kyaa aapko koii aur taKliif bhii hai?
(Q) you-to some more trouble also is

　　　　Have you got any other trouble?

When Waseem tells him he also has a cough **(mujhe khãasii bhii hai),** Dr Shah asks him if he's been out:

kal aap baahar gae?　Did you go out yesterday?
yesterday you outside gone

Waseem tells him:

mãi dost ke saath shaadii mẽ gayaa
I friend-with wedding-in gone

　　　　I went to a wedding with a friend.

Dr Shah tells him what's wrong:

aapko sardii lagii hai　You've caught a cold.
you-to cold struck is

CHECK-UP 2 How did Waseem catch cold?

3

When health visitor Yasmin Mengarmy came to call Zohra Nuzhai talked to her about her daughter Salma's ill health:

Yasmin:	Salma **(salmaa) kii tabiiyat Kharaab hai?**
Zohra:	**jii hãã. kaafii Kharaab hai.**
Yasmin:	**kyaa baat hai?**
Zohra:	**isko buKhaar hai, khããsii hai, galaa bhii Kharaab hai.**
Yasmin:	**kyaa aaj isne khaanaa khaayaa?**
Zohra:	**jii nahĩĩ, khaanaa to nahĩĩ khaayaa. thoRaa duudh hii piyaa.**
Yasmin:	**dekhiye, iske liye kuchh davaaii chaahiye. aap DaakTar kii** surgery **jaaiye.**

NOTES

Yasmin asks if Salma is ill:
Salma **kii tabiiyat Kharaab hai?**
Salma -of health   bad   is
                                 Salma's not well?

She asks if she's eaten anything today:
kyaa aaj isne   khaanaa khaayaa?
(Q)   today she-agent* food   eaten
                              Has she eaten today?

* See How the Language Works for notes on this 'special agent'.

Zohra tells her what she's had:
khaanaa to   nahĩĩ khaayaa...
food   as for not   eaten
                        Well she hasn't eaten...
...thoRaa duudh hii   piyaa. ... she's just had a little milk.
little   milk   only drunk

Yasmin suggests Zohra should get some medicine and tells her where to go for it:
dekhiye. iske liye kuchh davaaii chaahiye.
please look her-for   some   medicine is desirable/required
                        Look, you need some medicine
                        for her.
aap DaakTar kii surgery **jaaiye**
you doctor   -of surgery please go
                        Go to your surgery.

Remember that **dekhiye** and **jaaiye** have an inherent 'please' and so sound less abrupt than the English 'Look!' or 'Go!'

CHECK-UP 3 What's wrong with Salma? What has she had to eat or drink today?

KEYWORDS

△	**baat** (f)	matter/thing/problem
△	**peT** (m)	stomach
△	**dard** (m)	pain
△	**thoRaa/thoRii**	a little/few
△	**saa/sii**	'-ish'
△	**buKhaar** (m)	temperature/fever
△	**sar** (m)	head
△	**sar-dard** (m)	headache
△	**galaa** (m)	throat
△	**Kharaab**	bad
△	**khãã̃sii** (f)	cough
△.	**kal**	yesterday
△	**thii**	was (feminine)
△	**magar**	but
△	**aaj**	today
△	**koii**	some
△	**taKliif** (f)	problem/difficulty/trouble
△	**gae**	gone (masculine plural)
△	**dost** (m)	friend
△	**ke saath**	with
△	**shaadii** (f)	wedding
△	**sardii** (f)	cold
△	**lag**	'strike'
△	**lagii**	'struck' (feminine sing.)
△	**tabiiyat** (f)	health
△	**kaafii**	quite
△	**ne**	'agent' postposition
△	**khaanaa** (m)	food
△	**khaa**	eat
△	**khaayaa**	eaten (masculine sing.)
△	**duudh** (m)	milk
△	**pii**	drink
△	**piyaa**	drunk (masculine sing.)
△	**dekh**	look/see
△	**ke liye**	for
△	**iske liye**	for her/him
△	**kuchh**	some
△	**davaaii** (f)	medicine

SOUND SYSTEMS

r, R, AND Rh

The most important thing to remember about **r** in Hindi and Urdu is that *wherever* you see it written you should *pronounce* it. For most English speakers this can be a problem, as in words like 'farm' or 'car' the r is usually silent. The Hindi and Urdu **r** is more like a Scottish than an English r, made by lightly tapping the tongue against the ridge behind the teeth, so the word **magar** sounds very like a Scottish pronunciation of 'mugger'.

R and **Rh** are formed quite differently however. They are *retroflex* sounds (like **T** and **D** – see Unit 4) produced by lightly tapping the *underside* of the tongue against the *roof* of the mouth.

HOW THE LANGUAGE WORKS

'IS' AND 'WAS'

hũũ/hai/hãĩ (am/is/are) which we learnt right at the beginning in Unit 1, are all *present tense* forms – when Naheed says **mujhe sardard** *hai* she means that she has a headache *right now*, at the very time of speaking. But to say how you *were* feeling some time ago you have to use the *past tense* forms of **hũũ/hai/hãĩ** – **thaa/the/thii/thĩĩ**. Remember how Mrs Aggarwal described her symptoms:

kal	mujhe	thoRii sii	khããsii	*thii*
yesterday	to me	little-ish	cough	*was*

Yesterday I *had* a slight cough.

She uses **thii** instead of **hai** because she is describing how she *was* feeling before, not how she *is* feeling *now*.

'Was' and 'were' are the closest English equivalents of **thaa/the/thii/thĩĩ,** but notice that there are different masculine and feminine, as well as singular and plural forms:

	masculine	feminine	
sing.	**mãĩ thaa**	**mãĩ thii**	I was
	tuu thaa	**tuu thii**	You were (very familiar)
	ye/vo thaa		He/it was
		ye/vo thii	She/it was
plural	**ham the**	**ham thĩĩ**	We were
	tum the	**tum thĩĩ**	You were (familiar)
	ye/vo the	**ye/vo thĩĩ**	They were
	aap the	**aap thĩĩ**	You were (polite)

khãasii is feminine singular, which is why Mrs Aggarwal used **thii** rather than **thaa**.

Like **hũu/hai/hãi, thaa/the/thii/thĩi** may also be combined with a **-taa** form verb. So, as **mãi** Mohammed Ali **ko jaantaa hũu** means 'I *know* Mohammed Ali', **mãi** Mohammed Ali **ko jaantaa** *thaa* means 'I *knew* Mohammed Ali', or 'I *used to know* Mohammed Ali'.

'MISSION ACCOMPLISHED' – THE HINDI AND URDU -aa FORM

Up until this unit, all the verbs you have learnt (except for **hũu/hai/hãi**) have been either in the 'ongoing' **-taa** form or the polite request **-iye** form. In this unit, a new form has been introduced which refers to *completed* actions or events – the **-aa** form. When Waseem says **mãi dost ke saath shaadii mẽ** *gayaa* – 'I *went* to a wedding with a friend' – you know that he is talking about an event which is now over. Similarly, Yasmin and Zohra are talking about what Salma has had to eat or drink *earlier on today*, not about something she hasn't yet finished – **kyaa aaj isne khaanaa** *khaayaa*? – 'Has she *eaten* today?' **thoRaa duudh hii** *piyaa* – '(She's) just *drunk* a little milk', or '(She) just *drank* a little milk.'

Like the **-taa** form (Unit 2 – How The Language Works) the **-aa** form has different masculine and feminine, and singular and plural forms:

	singular	plural
masculine	**-aa***	**-e**
feminine	**-ii**	**-ĩi****

* **-aa** generally becomes **-yaa** when preceded by a vowel.
** **-ĩi** becomes **-ii** if followed by **hãi** or **thĩi**.

You can see that the endings themselves are not at all difficult to learn if you have already learnt the **-taa** form – just take away the **t** and you're left with the **-aa** form! All you have to do is add it to the verb stem. For example **khaayaa** ('eaten') is formed by adding the masculine singular **-aa** to the verb stem **khaa** ('eat') and inserting the **y** because **khaa** ends in a vowel. There are a few irregular forms, the most common of which are listed at the back of the book. We've come across one already – **jaa + -aa** becomes **gayaa/gae/gaii/gaĩi**.

SPECIAL AGENTS

Unfortunately the rules for actually choosing *which* ending to use are slightly more complicated, and sometimes require you to use a 'special agent' postposition – **ne** – which really has no close equivalent in English at all.

With some verbs the **-aa** form agrees with the 'subject' of the sentence, just like the **-taa** form. (Have a look at Unit 2 again if you want reminding about this.) These are verbs like **jaa** ('go') or **aa** ('come') which take no direct object – what linguists call 'intransitive' verbs. That's why Waseem used the masculine singular **gayaa** when he said he'd been to a wedding – **mãĩ ... shaadii mẽ gayaa** – because he himself was the masculine singular subject of the sentence and there was no direct object. Here are some other examples, from when Dr Shah was talking to Waseem:

	Subject	Verb	
kal	**aap** (masc. pl.)	**baahar gae?** (masc. pl.)	Did you go out yesterday?
aapko	**sardii** (fem. sing.)	**lagii hai** (fem. sing.)	You've caught a cold.

Beware that *intransitive* sentences in Hindi and Urdu may sometimes be *transitive* in English! In Hindi and Urdu a cold strikes *to* you (**aapko**) so there is no direct object in this sentence, whereas in English you actively and directly catch a cold.

In sentences where there *is* a direct object (in which the verb is 'transitive') the rules of agreement of an **-aa** form verb are different. Generally speaking the verb agrees with the *direct object* and not with the word which would be considered the 'subject' in the equivalent English sentence. In addition this 'subject' is marked with the 'special agent' postposition **ne**, and so is actually in the *oblique* form. So, when Yasmin asked if Salma had eaten anything – **kyaa aaj isne khaanaa khaayaa?**, ('Has she eaten food today?') **khaayaa** is actually *masculine* singular to agree with the masculine singular direct object **khaanaa** ('food'), and *not* with the feminine 'subject' ('she') – the person who does the actual eating. 'She' (**ye**) in fact must become oblique **is** because it is followed by **ne**, the word which shows who is the 'doer' – the 'agent'.

That may all sound rather complicated. It's certainly quite different from the way English and many other European languages work, and it may take you a little time to get used to it. But it's not as difficult as it may at first appear. Here are some more examples:

Subject	Direct Object	Verb	
Salma **ne** (fem. sing.)	**duudh** (masc. sing.)	**piyaa** (masc. sing.)	Salma drank some milk.
Naveed **ne** (masc. sing.)	**chaaval** (masc. pl.)	**khaae hãĩ** (masc. pl.)	Naveed has eaten the rice.
Waseem **ne** (masc. sing.)	**sabziyãã** (fem. pl.)	**khaaii thĩĩ** (fem. pl.)	Waseem had eaten the vegetables.

You can see from these examples that the **-aa** form, like the **-taa** form, can also be combined with **hai** or **thaa**. The number of possible combinations and the subtly different meanings they have is quite high, certainly more than can be covered in a book of this size, but if you look in the grammatical summary at the back you will find some of the most common combinations listed. You will also find a list of special oblique pronoun forms that go with 'special agent' **ne**.

'A HEADACHE IS TO ME.'

Remember that the subject of a Hindi or Urdu sentence may not be exactly the same thing as the subject of an equivalent sentence in English. When you talk about mental and physical states over which you have no control (such as headaches or hunger) it is generally the headache or the hunger that is the 'subject' in Hindi and Urdu:

mujhe sar-dard hai   I have a headache.
To me   headache is.

hii, bhii, to, saa

These four words of Hindi and Urdu are called *particles* and are used to give a particular nuance to a sentence. This makes them difficult to translate precisely. These particles always *follow* the words they qualify:

hii – 'exclusive' particle:

The nearest equivalent in English is 'only'. **mujhe paalak hii chaahiye** – 'I want only spinach' (and I'm not at all interested in coriander, fenugreek, or anything else you've got to offer).

bhii – 'inclusive' particle:

The nearest equivalent in English is 'also' or 'as well'. **kyaa aapko buKhaar bhii hai?** – 'Have you got a fever as well?' (in addition to all the other ailments you've already told me about).

to – 'as for' particle:

to can only be roughly translated into English as 'as far as X is concerned' or 'as for X'. **khaanaa to isne nahĩĩ khaayaa** – 'As for food, well he hasn't eaten anything'.

saa – '-ish' particle:

saa is placed after an adjective to modify its meaning. It changes its form to agree with the adjective – **se** (masculine plural) and **sii** (feminine):

baRaa saa kamraa   a 'largish' room
chhoTii sii khiRkii   a 'smallish' window

EXERCISES

1

Aches and pains

These people are in pain. What are they saying? Fill in the blanks following the example.

a **mujhe khãẫsii hai**   *b* _____

_____   *d* _____

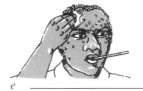

e _____

2

Doctor doctor

Harbans Kaur's young son Jaswinder is not feeling well so she takes him to Dr Patel. Jaswinder has a cough. He had a slight temperature yesterday, but it's gone today. He had too much pilao for lunch yesterday and has a stomach ache as well. How does Harbans answer Dr Patel's questions?

Dr Patel: **iskii tabiiyat kaisii hai?**

Harbans Kaur: _____

Dr Patel: **kyaa baat hai?**

Harbans Kaur: _____

Dr Patel: **achchhaa, khãẫsii. kyaa isko buKhaar bhii hai?**

Harbans Kaur: _____

Dr Patel: **kyaa isko koii aur taKliif bhii hai?**

Harbans Kaur: _____

Dr Patel: **kal isne kyaa khaayaa?**

Harbans Kaur: _____

3
Go-between

Mrs Williams, a health visitor, has come to see Mrs Begum, your neighbour. Mrs Begum asks you to help her talk to her.

a   Mrs Williams asks you to ask Mrs Begum how she is. What do you say?

b   Mrs Begum says **mãĩ Thiik nahĩĩ hũũ**. Mrs Williams wants to know what's the matter. What do you say?

c   Mrs Begum says **mere peT mẽ dard hai**. Mrs Williams wants to know what she had to eat yesterday. What do you say?

d   Mrs Begum says **kal mãĩne kuchh nahĩĩ khaayaa. meraa galaa Kharaab thaa**. Mrs Williams wants to know if she has any other symptoms. What do you say?

e   Mrs Begum says **mujhe thoRii khããsii bhii hai**. Mrs Williams wants to know if she has a headache as well. What do you say?

f   Mrs Begum says **jii hãã, mujhe sar-dard bhii hai**. Mrs Williams wants to know if she has a temperature as well. What do you say?

4
'Was' or 'were'?

Here are some unfinished sentences. Complete them with one of the words in the right hand column.

a   **kal mujhe thoRii khããsii** _____.

b   **uskaa naam jamilaa** _____.

c   **merii beTiyãã paakistaan mẽ** _____.

d   **ham vahãã kaam karte** _____.   thaa

e   **aapke bhaaii kaise** _____?   the

f   **mujhe buKhaar** _____.   thii

g   **meraa galaa bhii Kharaab** _____.   thĩĩ

h   **uskii tabiiyat Thiik nahĩĩ** _____.

i   **aap kahãã rahtii** _____?

j   **kamre mẽ ek hii khiRkii** _____.

5
kal aapne kyaa khaayaa?

What did you eat yesterday? Fill the gaps and remember to choose the right form of **-aa/-e/-ii/-ĩĩ**. The first one is done for you.

a   **kal mãĩne <u>chaaval</u> khaae.**

plain rice

pilau rice

b   **kal mãĩne** _____ **khaa__.**

c   **kal mãĩne** _____ **khaa__.**

pakoras

d **kal mãine** _____ **khaa__.**

yoghurt

e

kal mãine _____ **khaa__.**

f **kal mãine** _____ **khaa__.**

6

Whither away?

Amar Nath has a well-travelled family. His brothers, sisters, sons, and daughters are spread around the globe. He starts telling a friend where they've gone. See if you can finish the story for him. Remember to use the right form of **-aa/-e/-ii/-ı̃**.

a **meraa beTaa** Ramesh Scotland **gayaa hai.**
b **merii baRii bahan** _____ Canada _____ _____.
c **mere baRe bhaaii** _____ Japan _____ _____.
d **merii beTii** _____ India _____ _____.
e **meraa chhoTaa bhaaii** _____ Fiji _____ _____.
f **merii chhoTii bahan** _____ Trinidad _____ _____.

7
Missing particles

Fill in the gaps with **hii, bhii, to,** or **saa.**

merii ek _____ bahan hãĩ. mere do bhaaii _____ hãĩ. mere bhaaii _____ Bradford **mẽ rahte hãĩ magar mãĩ** Cambridge **mẽ rahtii hũũ.** merii bahan _____ yahãã Cambridge **mẽ** _____ rahtii hãĩ. merii bahan kii tabiiyat Thiik hai, magar mujhe thoRaa _____ buKhaar hai. mujhe thoRii _____ khããsii _____ hai.

8
Listening exercise

Here are three different people talking to their doctor. Listen to them describing their complaints. On the chart below tick off their symptoms.

	1	2	3
Temperature			
Sore throat			
Headache			
Cough			
Stomach ache			

BACKGROUND

POPULAR MUSIC

Most Hindi and Urdu films are musicals, and film songs account for most of the light popular music in Hindi and Urdu. In view of the enormous output of Hindi and Urdu films, and hence songs, the actual number of major recording artists is surprisingly small. But these few 'playback singers' are as much a focus of media interest and popular adulation as the film stars themselves. Great names of the past include Mohammed Rafi, Mukesh, and Kishore Kumar, while the remarkable sisters Lata Mangeshkar and Asha Bhosle continue to record and perform. They are reputed to be the most prolific recording artists in the world.

Records and cassettes featuring these artists are easily obtainable in many Asian music stores, in a variety of formats. You can buy film sound-tracks, or compilations featuring a particular singer, or recordings of live performances. Many singers tour Britain quite

frequently, so you might like to take the opportunity to see them performing live as well.

The language of the songs is often quite poetic and so not easy for a learner to follow, but some lyrics are quite straightforward. This classic from 'Shri 420' (starring Raj Kapoor) was sung by Mukesh:

meraa juutaa hai jaapaanii
my   shoe   is   Japanese

ye   patluun inglistaanii
these trousers English

sar   pe laal Topii ruusii
head-on red hat   Russian

phir bhii dil   hai hindustaanii
   but   heart is   Hindustani

In Britain itself the 1980s saw interesting developments with the emergence of young 'home-grown' talents trying out new musical and lyrical styles. Nazia Hassan's 'Disco Deewane' made a considerable impact at the beginning of the decade, and she and her brother Zoheb have produced a number of LP's since then, singing in Urdu. However, Punjabi Bhangra, often with a disco flavour, is probably most widely popular as dance music with young Asians in Britain.

kyaa aapko angrezii aatii hai?

TALKING ABOUT LANGUAGE

TALKING ABOUT LEARNING

SAYING WHAT YOU CAN DO

1

At this parent-teacher meeting in a Glasgow school, teacher Mrs Nizami finds one parent who doesn't speak English:

Mrs Nizami:	**kyaa aapko hindii yaa urduu aatii hai?**
Mr Virdee:	**jii hã͠a, donõ aatii hã͠i.**
Mrs Nizami:	**aapke bachche kaa naam kyaa hai?**
Mr Virdee:	Jasbir Singh (**jasbiir sing**).
Mrs Nizami:	**achchhaa**, Jasbir.
Mr Virdee:	**paRhaaii mẽ kaisaa hai?**
Mrs Nizami:	**kaafii mehnat kar rahaa hai, aur achchhe nambar le rahaa hai.**

NOTES

Mrs Nizami asks Mr Virdee if he knows Hindi or Urdu:
kyaa aapko hindii yaa urduu aatii   hai?
(Q)   you-to Hindi or   Urdu   coming is

Do you know Hindi or Urdu?

He tells her:
donõ aatii   hã͠i   I know both.
both   coming are

He asks about his son:
paRhaaii mẽ kaisaa hai?   How is he getting on at school?
studies   -in how   is

She tells him:
kaafii mehnat   kar rahaa hai He's working quite hard . . .
much   hard work do '-ing' is

aur achchhe nambar le   rahaa hai.
and good   marks   take '-ing' is

... and getting good marks.

CHECK-UP 1 Does Mr Virdee know only one Asian language?

2

Jenny Mears uses Hindi and Urdu in her English classes for adults.
One evening she had a new student:

Jenny: **aaj aap pahlii dafaa is klaas mẽ aaii hãi, na?**
Student: **jii hãã. kyaa aapko urduu aatii hai?**
Jenny: **bahut kam aatii hai. mãi bol saktii hũũ. thoRii paRh bhii saktii hũũ.**
Student: **kyaa aap likh bhii saktii hãi?**
Jenny: **jii? phir kahiye.**
Student: **kyaa aap urduu likh saktii hãi?**
Jenny: **jii nahĩĩ. mãi hindii likh saktii hũũ. magar urduu mẽ apnaa naam hii likh saktii hũũ.**

NOTES

First Jenny checks she's new:

aaj aap pahlii dafaa is   klaas mẽ aaii hãi, na?
today you first   time this class-in come are (tag)

This is the first time you've
come to this class, isn't it?

na is a word you can 'tag' on to any sentence to make it a question – a
bit like 'isn't it?', or 'don't you?', in English.

Jenny modestly says she knows very little Urdu:

(mujhe urduu) bahut kam aatii   hai.
to me   Urdu   very   less   coming is
                              I know very little (Urdu).

mãĩ bol   saktii hũ̃.   I can speak it.
I   speak   can

thoRii paRh bhii saktii hũ̃.   I can also read a little.
little   read   also   can

Her student asks about her writing skills:

kyaa aap likh bhii saktii hãĩ? Can you write as well?
(Q)   you   write   also   can

But Jenny doesn't follow the question:

jii?   phir kahiye.   Sorry, could you repeat that
(respect) again please say   please?

Jenny can write Hindi (**mãĩ hindii likh saktii hũ̃**), but is not so good in Urdu:

urduu mẽ apnaa naam hii   likh   saktii hũ̃.
Urdu   -in 'my'   name   only write   can
                              I can just write my name in
                              Urdu.

CHECK-UP 2 Is Jenny better at writing or speaking Urdu?

3

Sneh talked to student Fahmeeda Yamin about the languages she knew, and how long she had been learning:

Sneh:	**aapko kitnii zabaanē aatii hāī?**
Fahmeeda:	**chaar. panjaabii, urduu, hindii, aur angrezii. ab mãĩ** German **siikh rahii hũũ.**
Sneh:	German **kab se siikh rahii hāī?**
Fahmeeda:	**tiin saal se.**
Sneh:	**kyaa aap** German **bol saktii hāī?**
Fahmeeda:	**jii hãã. hamaare Tiichar ne hamē kaafii** German **sikhaa dii hai.**
Sneh:	**achchhaa. kyaa aap** German **paRh bhii saktii hāī?**
Fahmeeda:	**jii hãã. mãĩne** course **kii pahlii tiin kitaabē paRh lii hāī.**

NOTES

Sneh asks Fahmeeda how many languages she knows:

aapko kitnii   zabaanē* aatii   hāī?
you-to how many languages   coming are

                              How many languages do you
* Hindi **bhaashaaē**   know?

Fahmeeda tells her which language she's learning now:
ab   mãĩ German **siikh rahii hũũ.**
now I   German learn '-ing' am

                              Now I am learning German.

Sneh asks her how long she has been learning German:
(aap) German **kab se   siikh rahii hāī?**
you   German when from learn '-ing' are

                              How long have you been
                              learning German?

And Fahmeeda replies:
tiin   saal se   For three years.
three years from

She says how much her teacher has taught them and how many books she's read:
hamaare Tiichar ne hamē kaafii German **sikhaa dii   hai**
our   teacher   agent to us much German teach 'given' is

                              Our teacher has taught us a lot
                              of German.

mãĩne course **kii pahlii tiin   kitaabē paRh lii   hāī.**
I agent course -of first   three   books   read 'taken' are

                              I've read the first three course
                              books.

CHECK-UP 3 Can Fahmeeda speak as well as read German?

KEYWORDS

△	**yaa**	or
△	**donõ**	both
△	**paRhaaii** (f)	studies/education
△	**kaafii**	quite/much
△	**mehnat** (f)	hard work
△	**rahaa**	'-ing' (masculine)
△	**achchhaa**	good
△	**nambar** (m)	number
△	**achchhe nambar**	good marks
△	**le**	take
△	**pahlaa**	first
△	**dafaa** (f)	time
△	**pahlii dafaa**	first time
△	**klaas** (f)	class
△	**na**	tag question
△	**bahut**	much/very
△	**kam**	less
△	**bahut kam**	very little
△	**bol**	speak
△	**sak**	can/be able
△	**mãi . . . saktii hũũ**	I can . . .
△	**paRh**	read
△	**likh**	write
△	**phir**	again
△	**kah**	say
△	**apnaa**	my/your/his/her etc.
△	**zabaan** (f)	language (Urdu)
△	**bhaashaa** (f)	language (Hindi)
△	**ab**	now
△	**siikh**	learn
△	**rahii**	'-ing' (feminine)
△	**kab**	when?
△	**saal** (m)	year
△	**hamẽ**	to us
△	**sikhaa**	teach
△	**de**	give
△	**dii**	given (feminine)
△	**kitaab** (f)	book
△	**lii**	taken (feminine)
△	**chiTThii** (f)	letter
△	**unhõne**	he/she/they (agent)

SOUND SYSTEMS

e AND o

English speakers of English tend to hear Hindi and Urdu **e** and **o** as being similar to the vowel sounds in 'lay' and 'low' respectively. If you use these *English* English vowel sounds in your Hindi and Urdu, people will probably understand you, but your foreign accent will be unmistakable. The English sounds are *diphthongs* – they start in one place in the mouth and finish somewhere else. The Hindi and Urdu sounds are *monophthongs* – the tongue keeps the same position all the way through the vowel, i.e. quite high and to the front of the mouth for **e**, and quite high but to the back for **o**. Once again most Scottish speakers of English have an advantage as they already have these sounds. So **le** rhymes with Scottish 'lay', and **lo** rhymes with Scottish 'low'.

HOW THE LANGUAGE WORKS

mujhe urduu aatii hai

The notion 'I know Urdu' can be expressed in Hindi and Urdu in two different ways:

mãĩ urduu jaantaa hũũ

I   Urdu   knowing am

Lit. I know Urdu.

But it is more common to say:

mujhe urduu aatii   hai

to me   Urdu   coming is

Lit. Urdu comes/is coming to me.

The two expressions are generally interchangeable when you talk about *skills* such as speaking a language, music, games etc. But since it is Urdu that is the 'subject' in the second expression, it is the language, rather than the person knowing the language, that is the focus of attention. However, when it is only *knowledge* that is being referred to (such as knowing a person) you must use the verb **jaan** 'know'.

STILL LEARNING

You will remember from Unit 2 that **mãĩ** Bordesley Green **mẽ rahtii hũũ** could mean 'I live in Bordesley Green' or 'I am living in Bordesley Green'. For Rena Azim, living in Bordesley Green is both a regular day-to-day reality ('habitual') and an ongoing process. (She'll still be there tomorrow.) It might seem a bit confusing that the same set of words in one language can be translated in more than one way into another, but if you stop and think about it it's really not so

surprising. Languages *are* different and they all shape the way we talk about things like time and space in subtly different ways.

This is particularly noticeable when the languages are as distantly related as English and Hindi and Urdu. In this unit we have learnt a new way of describing an ongoing activity:

vo kaafii mehnat kar rahaa hai   He's working quite hard.
aur (vo) achchhe nambar le   And (he) is getting good marks.
rahaa hai
ab mãi German **siikh rahii hũũ**   Now I'm learning German.

In each of these sentences a verb stem, **kar** ('do') **le** ('take'), **siikh** ('learn') is combined with **rahaa** (masc.) or **rahii** (fem.), followed by **hai** or **hũũ**. The sense this conveys is that the working or the getting or the learning is *still going on*. **rahaa, rahii,** and **rahe** (masc. pl.) literally mean 'stayed'. (They are in fact the **-aa** forms of **rah** ('stay').) But this particular combination with a preceding verb stem is very similar in meaning to English ongoing '-ing', which has a narrower focus than Hindi and Urdu **-taa**. It emphasises 'ongoingness' rather *habitual* or *uncompleted* activity, which the **-taa** form additionally conveys.

SINCE WHEN?

It would be nice to say that **siikh rahii hũũ** always means 'am learning'. Unfortunately, it's not quite true. There is one important exception which we have already come across. Remember how Sneh asked Fahmeeda how long she had been learning German, **(aap)** German **kab se siikh rahii hãi?**

This 'literally' translates as 'Since when are you learning German?', whereas the more natural English sentence would be 'How long *have you been learning* German?', using 'have you been learning' instead of 'are learning'. Notice also that Fahmeeda says the equivalent of '*From* (not *for*) three years'. If she had answered with a complete sentence she would have said **mãi tiin saal se siikh rahii hũũ** – 'I *have been learning* for three years'.

HELP YOURSELF?

Two new very important verbs have been introduced in this unit – **de** and **le**. As the *main* verb of a sentence **de** basically means 'give' and **le** 'take'. Remember what Mrs Nizami said about Jasbir: **(vo) achchhe nambar le rahaa hai** – 'He's taking (or getting) good marks'. In this sentence **le** itself is the main verb.

Another very common usage for both **le** and **de** is for them to be used to 'help' or 'support' *another* main verb. When Fahmeeda says **hamaare Tiichar ne hamẽ kaafii** German **sikhaa dii hai** ('Our

teacher has taught us a lot of German') the main verb in this sentence is **sikhaa** ('teach'). **dii**, the feminine singular -**aa** form of **de**, is here a 'helping' verb which gives an additional nuance of meaning to **sikhaa**. Using **de** as a 'helping' verb in this way conveys the meaning of 'doing something for someone else' – in the case of Fahmeeda's teacher 'giving the benefit' of teaching to Fahmeeda. Remember also from Unit 6 that when using the 'mission accomplished' -**aa** form you use **ne** to mark the 'special agent' – **hamaare Tiichar** – and the verb agrees with the direct *object* – feminine singular 'German'. All languages are feminine in Hindi and Urdu. (See the grammatical summary for the full list of -**aa** forms of **de** and **le**.)

le as a 'helping verb' often gives the meaning of 'doing something for oneself'. So, when Fahmeeda says **mãine** course **kii pahlii tiin kitaabẽ paRh lii hãĩ,** (**lii** being the feminine -**aa** form of **le** to agree with **kitaabẽ**) she is saying she has 'taken the benefit' of reading the first three course books.

CAN DO

To say you 'can do' something in Hindi and Urdu, you put the word for 'can' *after* the word for 'do':

mãĩ urduu bol   saktii hũũ   I can speak Urdu.
I   Urdu   speak   can

Note that **sak** is another 'helping' verb, which gives an extra nuance of 'ability' to the main verb, in this case **bol**. Unlike **le** and **de**, though, it can *never* stand on its own as a main verb itself. In English 'I can't' could be a complete sentence, but in Hindi and Urdu you must always say 'I can't *speak*' (**mãĩ nahĩĩ *bol* saktii**) or 'I can't *read*' (**mãĩ nahĩĩ *paRh* saktii**) etc.

apnaa naam – MY NAME, OR YOUR NAME?

In previous Units we've come across a number of words for describing who things belong to – **hamaaraa** – 'our', **uskaa** and **iskaa** – 'his' or 'her', **aapkaa** – 'your', and **meraa** – 'my'. (For the full list of possessives see the grammatical summary.) In this Unit we've learnt a new word, **apnaa**, which can mean any of these. Remember how Jenny said she could only write her name in Urdu: **urduu mẽ (mãĩ)** *apnaa* **naam hii likh saktii hũũ.**

Here **apnaa** means 'my', and it would have been wrong for Jenny to have used the word **meraa** (the only word we've learnt for 'my' so far) in this sentence. But if you wanted to ask someone if they could write their name, rather than telling them that you can write yours, you would use **apnaa** again, this time to mean 'your' – **kyaa aap** *apnaa* **naam likh sakte hãĩ?** – 'Can you write *your* name?'. And **vo** *apnaa* **naam likh saktaa hai** means 'He can write *his* name', where **apnaa** now means 'his'. Confused? Don't be – the basic rule is quite simple:

When the owner or 'possessor' of the thing you're talking about (for example 'name') is the *subject* of the sentence, be it 'I' or 'You', 'He' or 'She', then you show their ownership with **apnaa** – not with **meraa, aapkaa, uskaa** etc. So Jenny uses **apnaa** to mean 'my' because she herself (**mãĩ**) is the subject of the sentence.

EXERCISES

1

Cross purposes

There's a new student in the adult ESL class. The teacher tries to make her feel at home by speaking to her in Urdu. Can you re-order this conversation so that it makes sense.

Teacher

a **jii? phir kahiye.**
b **aapkaa naam kyaa hai?**
c **assalaam alaikum.**
d **kyaa aapko angrezii aatii hai?**
e **apnaa naam likh saktii hãĩ?**

Student

1 **jii hãã, likh saktii hũũ.**
2 **vaalaikum assalaam**
3 Asma Zahid.
4 **meraa naam** Asma Zahid **hai.**
5 **bahut kam aatii hai. mãĩ thoRii paRh saktii hũũ, magar bol nahĩĩ saktii.**

2

What do you know?

You're invited to a Hindu wedding, where you meet amongst the guests a man who's recently arrived from India.

a He seems surprised that you greeted him with **namaste**. Explain to him that you're learning Hindi.
b He asks how long you've been learning. Tell him that you've been learning for a year.
c He asks you another question, but you don't understand. Ask him to repeat it.
d He speaks more slowly and this time you follow. He wants to know if you can read Hindi. Tell him you can't but you can write your name.
e He asks how many languages you know. Tell him you know English and you also know a little Urdu.
f He asks who is coming to the wedding. Tell him you don't know and explain that this is the first Hindu wedding you've ever attended. (The Hindi for Hindu is **hinduu**.)

3
Can or can't?

Choosing from the list of verbs below and the appropriate masculine or feminine form of **saktaa/saktii**, describe the cartoons. The first two have been done for you.

paRh, bol, kar, siikh, likh, khaa

a   **ye urduu <u>paRh saktii</u> hai.**   *b*   **ye hindii nahı̃ı̃ <u>paRh saktii</u>.**

c   **iske peT mẽ dard hai. ye**   *d*   **iskaa galaa Kharaab hai. ye**
   _____ _____.   **_____ _____.**

e   **ye hindii _____ _____**   *f*   **ye kuchh _____ _____**
   _____.   **_____.**

g   **ye kaam _____ _____ _____.**

4
Action stations

In this station waiting-room above *everybody* is busy. Note down at least six different activities in as much detail as possible, e.g. Nazir **hindii kii kitaab paRh rahaa hai**. Here are some questions to start you off: Who's eating what? Who's speaking which language? Who's writing a letter (**chiTThii**) to whom? Remember to use the right **rahaa** form.

5
Odd one out

a   Which one of these is not a part of the body?

sar	**peT**	**galaa**	**dost**

b   Which one of these wouldn't you eat?

dhaniyaa	**paalak**	**kitaab**	**methii**

c   Which of these doesn't ask for an answer?

kaisaa	**kal**	**kahā̃**	**kab**

d   Which of these could be anywhere?

kitaab	**saamne**	**niiche**	**uupar**

e   Which of these requires no interpretation?

bol	**khaa**	**likh**	**paRh**

f   Which of these can never be independent?

aataa hū̃	**jaataa hū̃**	**rahtaa hū̃**	**saktaa hū̃**

6
Give and take

Following the example, fill in the captions to these pictures. Remember to choose the appropriate **-aa** form of either **le** or **de**:–

a

mãĩne khaanaa khaa liyaa hai.

b

mãĩne Anita **ko chiTThii likh dii hai.**

c   **mãine duudh _____ _____ _____.**

d   **mãine kitaab _____ _____ _____.**

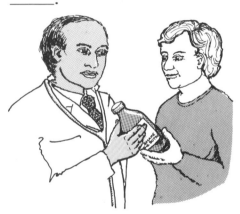

Thank you Ravinder

e   **mãine DaakTar se davaaii _____ _____ _____.**

f   Ravinder **ne mere liye bahut mehnat _____ _____ _____.**

g   **Tiichar ne mujhe kitaab _____ _____ _____.**

h   **mãine apnaa kaam _____ _____ _____.**

7

Mm . . . mm . . . mm . . . mm . . .

mã̃ı, mã̃ıne, mujhe, meraa, mere, merii are all to do with 'me'. The speaker here has a headache and a sore throat. Fill in the gaps with words beginning with m.

kal m_____ DaakTar ke paas gaii. unhõne m_____ kuchh davaaii de dii thii. m_____ kuchh kaam kiyaa thaa, magar aaj m_____ nahĩ̃ kar saktii. aaj m_____ sar-dard hai. m_____ buKhaar hai aur m_____ galaa bhii Kharaab hai. m_____ bol bhii nahĩ̃ saktii. m_____ khaanaa chaahiye magar m_____ restaurant nahĩ̃ jaa saktii.

8

Listening exercise

Here are three learners of Hindi and Urdu talking about themselves. Note down as much information as possible about them:– their names, where they live, what they do, as well as how long they've been learning, whether they can read or write etc.

BACKGROUND

SERIOUS MUSIC

The Indian musical tradition is as old as the Indus Valley civilisation. All the religious poetry and a great deal of secular poetry written in India since the Vedas (*c.* 2000 BC) is meant to be sung. The Indian word 'sangit', usually translated as 'music', originally referred to a combination of vocal music, instrumental music and dance.

The Indian musical scale is more or less the same as the diatonic scale used in the West. But Indian music is melody-based unlike harmony-based Western classical music. A certain combination of notes with a definite ascending and descending order is known as a *raga*. There are hundreds of simple and complicated *ragas* which are sung or played on instruments in the Indian sub-continent. Folk tunes associated with certain regions and modes of singing also exist, and some of these folk tunes have assumed the status of *ragas*.

The various types of beats of percussion instruments like Tabla (North Indian) and Mridangam (South Indian) are called *bols*. Dance rhythms also have their *bols*, which are spoken rhythmically as accompaniment to classical dances such as Kathak.

Since the beginning of the Muslim period in Indian history (the time of Amir Khusro) there have been two major musical traditions in

India – the Hindustani or the North Indian and the Karnatic or the South Indian. Though the underlying structure of the *ragas* and rhythms of both the traditions is the same, the North Indian (or Hindustani) tradition has been influenced by the Persian, Turkish and Central Asian musical traditions. Amir Khusro, the first major writer who wrote in Hindi and Urdu, contributed enormously to the Hindustani tradition by expounding its theory, inventing new styles of singing and musical instruments and modifying some existing ones.

With regard to vocal music, there are a number of performers who sing in Hindi and Urdu in the various different genres and who regularly tour Britain or whose recordings are easily obtainable from music stores.

One of the most popular genres is ghazal (pronounced as **Gazal**). The term ghazal actually refers to a particular form of Urdu poetry which has strict metrical conventions. The best known ghazal singers of today are Mehdi Hasan and Ghulam Ali from Pakistan, and Anup Jalota, Pankaj Udhas, Jagjit Singh and his wife Chitra Singh from India. They all compose their music in *ragas*. Some young British-based artists such as Najma Akhtar have also introduced new ideas and influences into ghazal singing.

The qawali style of singing, believed to have been invented by Amir Khusro, is the most popular form of group singing in North India and Pakistan. In a qawali, a devotional song or an Urdu ghazal is sung in some *raga*. The style of singing is rhythmical, accompanied by drum beats and the clapping of hands. Nusrat Fateh Ali Khan's qawali group from Pakistan is the best known in the West. They sing in both Urdu and Punjabi.

Left: Shankar Ghosh playing the tabla and Shujaat Husain Khan on the sitar; right: Kathak dancing performed by Alpana Sengupta. It is a form of telling stories from the religious epics and its main feature is the intricate and amazingly fast footwork which follows strict rhythmic patterns.

aapke kyaa kyaa shauK haĩ?

TALKING ABOUT HOBBIES AND INTERESTS

EXPRESSING LIKES AND DISLIKES

1

Sneh and Omar asked several people (including each other) about their hobbies and interests:

Sneh:	Savita, **(savitaa) aapke kyaa kyaa shauK haĩ?**
Savita:	**mujhe giTaar bajaane kaa shauK hai.**
Sneh:	Omar, **aapke kyaa kyaa shauK haĩ?**
Omar:	**mujhe fuTbaal khelne kaa shauK hai.**
Omar:	**aapke kyaa kyaa shauK haĩ?**
Abdul Gulzar:	**mujhe tairne kaa shauK hai.**
Mohammed Bashir:	**mujhe kitaabẽ paRhne kaa shauK hai.**
Rama Sharma:	**mujhe gaane kaa shauK hai.**
Nazreen Butt:	**mujhe ghuumne-phirne kaa shauK hai.**
Omar:	**aapke kyaa kyaa shauK haĩ?**
Daahyanti Mistry:	**mujhe** badminton **khelnaa pasand hai.**

NOTES

If you want to ask what someone's hobbies are, you can say:
aapke kyaa kyaa shauK haĩ? What are your hobbies/
your   what what interests are   interests?

You can reply like this:
mujhe giTaar bajaane kaa shauK hai
to me   guitar   playing   -of interest is

                   My hobby is playing the guitar.

Or like this:
mujhe badminton **khelnaa pasand hai.**
to me   badminton playing   likeable is

                   I like playing badminton.

You can also say **mujhe** badminton **khelne kaa shauK hai**. This would imply that you not only like playing badminton but you also play it regularly.

CHECK-UP 1 Who likes walking? (Check *Keywords*)

2

Omar asked Manjit Kaur Rauni and Dayal Sharma what sorts of things they liked:

Omar:	Manjit **(manjiit) jii, aapke kyaa kyaa shauK hãi?**
Manjit:	**mujhe khaanaa banaane kaa shauK hai.**
Omar:	**aapko kis Kism kaa khaanaa pasand hai?**
Manjit:	**mujhe hindustaanii khaanaa pasand hai. magar zyaadaa mirch-masaalaa pasand nahĩi.**
Omar:	Sharma **(sharmaa) jii aapke kyaa kyaa shauK hãi?**
Mr Sharma:	Omar **saahab, mujhe filmẽ dekhne kaa shauK hai.**
Omar:	**aapko kis Kism kii filmẽ pasand hãi?**
Mr Sharma:	**mujhe urduu aur hindii filmẽ pasand hãi.**

Omar:	**kyaa aapko sangiit bhii pasand hai?**
Mr Sharma:	**jii hãã, bahut pasand hai.**
Omar:	**aapko kis Kism kaa sangiit pasand hai?**
Mr Sharma:	**mujhe klaasiikii muusiiKii Khaas taur par pasand hai.**

NOTES

Omar asks Manjit about the kind of food she likes:
aapko kis   Kism kaa khaanaa pasand hai?
you-to what type -of food   likeable is
                                 What kind of food do you like?

She tells him:
mujhe hindustaanii khaanaa pasand hai
to me   Indian   food   likeable is
                                 I like Indian food.
magar zyaadaa mirch-masaalaa pasand nahĩĩ.
but   much   spices   likeable not
                                 But I don't like a lot of spices.

Omar asks Mr Sharma what sorts of films and music he likes:
aapko kis   Kism kii filmẽ pasand hãĩ?
you-to what type -of films likeable are
                                 What kind of films do you like?
aapko kis   Kism kaa sangiit pasand hai?
you-to what type -of music likeable is
                                 What kind of music do you like?

Mr Sharma says he likes music very much (**bahut pasand hai**), *particularly* classical music:
mujhe klaasiikii muusiiKii Khaas taur par pasand hai.
to me   classical music   especially   likeable is
                                 I especially like classical music.

CHECK-UP 2 What sort of films does Mr Sharma like?

3

Out walking in the park Omar asked Jasbinder Sanim what she thought of the cold weather:

Omar:	**aapko ye sardii kaa mausam achchhaa yaa buraa lagtaa hai?**
Jasbinder:	**sardii achchhii nahĩĩ lagtii hai.**
Omar:	**aur garmii kaa mausam?**
Jasbinder:	**bahut achchhaa lagtaa hai.**

NOTES

Omar asks Jasbinder whether she *likes* or *dislikes* the cold:

aapko ye sardii kaa mausam achchhaa yaa buraa lagtaa
you-to this cold -of weather good   or bad   striking
hai?   Do you like or dislike this cold
is   weather?

The difference between **buraa lagtaa hai** and **pasand nahīī hai** is
the same as that between 'dislike' and 'don't like' in English.

He asks her about hot weather too:
aur garmii kaa mausam?   And the hot weather?
and heat   -of weather

CHECK-UP 3 Does Jasbinder prefer hot or cold weather?

KEYWORDS

△	**shauK** (m)	interest/hobby
△	**giTaar** (m)	guitar
△	**bajaa**	play (instrument)
△	**bajaanaa** (m)	playing
△	**bajaane kaa shauK**	interest in playing
△	**fuTbaal** (m)	football
△	**khel**	play (game)
△	**khelnaa** (m)	playing
△	**tair**	swim
△	**tairnaa** (m)	swimming
△	**paRhnaa** (m)	reading
△	**gaa**	sing
△	**gaanaa** (m)	singing/song
△	**ghuumnaa-phirnaa** (m)	walking/strolling
△	**pasand**	likeable
△	**banaa**	make/prepare
△	**kis**	what (oblique)
△	**Kism** (f)	type/sort
△	**hindustaanii**	Indian
△	**zyaadaa**	a lot
△	**filmẽ** (f)	films
△	**sangiit** (m)	music
△	**klaasiikii muusiiKii** (f)	classical music
△	**Khaas taur par**	especially
△	**mausam** (m)	weather
△	**buraa**	bad
△	**sardii** (f)	cold
△	**garmii** (f)	heat
△	**sun**	hear/listen to
△	**sharaab** (f)	alcoholic drink
△	**tumhaaraa**	your (familiar)

SOUND SYSTEMS

k AND K

Some people make a distinction between the **k** of **kis** and the **K** of **Kism**, and some people don't. The **K** sound is actually only found in words borrowed from Arabic, so Urdu speakers may be rather more conscious of it than Hindi speakers. There is no sound like it in English, but if you want to pronounce it properly you have to make it

even further back in the mouth than **k**, virtually where mouth and throat meet, in fact. If this seems like too much effort few speakers of Hindi and Urdu will object if you use **k** instead (though remember that this is a different sound from English k: see Unit 5).

HOW THE LANGUAGE WORKS

'SEEING IS BELIEVING' – HINDI AND URDU -naa FORM

In English you create what is called a 'verbal noun' by adding '-ing' to the verb stem. The '-ing' forms 'seeing' and 'believing' in 'Seeing is believing' are nouns. 'Seeing' is actually the *subject* of the sentence. In Hindi and Urdu, you add **-naa** to the verb stem to create the verbal noun. This noun, like any other masculine noun ending in **-aa**, has both direct and oblique forms:

mujhe giTaar bajaanaa achchhaa lagtaa hai
to me   guitar   playing   good   seeming is
I like playing the guitar.

Here, **giTaar bajaanaa** is the subject of the sentence and so is in the direct form. **achchhaa** and **lagtaa** are in the masculine singular forms to agree with **bajaanaa**.

kyaa aapko angrezii sangiit sunne   kaa shauK hai?
Q   you-to English   music   listening -of interest is
Do you like listening to English music?

Here **sunnaa** is followed by the postposition **kaa** and so is in the oblique form.

kyaa/kis/kaun

kyaa 'what' and **kaun** 'who' differ in meaning exactly as their English translations do. **kaun** refers to persons and **kyaa** to things and often animals. **kis** is the oblique form (used before a postposition) of *both* **kaun** and **kyaa**, as in:

kal   yahãã kaun aayaa?   Who came here yesterday?
yesterday here   who   came

ye kitaab kis ne   paRhii hai?
this book   who (agent) read   is
Who has read this book?

aapko kyaa chaahiye?   What do you want?
you-to what desirable/required

merii kitaab kis   kamre mẽ hai?
my   book   what room -in is
In which room is my book?

kyaa kyaa

Words are repeated in Hindi and Urdu to convey many different types of meanings. Most commonly, repetition signifies a large number or great quantity or quality.

aapke kyaa kyaa shauK hãi? What are your interests?
you-of what what interests are

The speaker assumes that the addressee has many *different types of* hobbies or interests.

lagnaa

The verb **lag** means 'strike' or 'get attached'. (Remember **aapko sardii lagii hai** in Unit 6.) But when it is used for expressing likes and dislikes, it is more sensible to translate it as 'seem'.

mujhe	**hindustaanii**	**khaanaa**	**achchhaa**	**lagtaa**	**hai**
to me	Indian	food	good	seeming	is

Indian food seems good to me.
I like Indian food.

In Unit 9 we will find yet another meaning of **lag**.

WALKIE-TALKIE HINDI AND URDU

It is a common feature of the languages spoken in the Indian subcontinent to combine two words which are either similar in meaning or similar in sound (preferably both). The meaning of the compound expression in Hindi and Urdu is usually deliberately vague and unspecific. Very often, the second member of the compound is a rhyming or similar-sounding nonsense word. **ghuumnaa-phirnaa** is one example, and, of course, **bol-chaal** is another.

ghuum phir   move about, stroll
rotate   move around

bol   chaal   conversation, spoken language
words movement

Note that **bol-chaal** doesn't mean conversation in the sense of 'Yesterday I was having a conversation with my neighbour about the weather'. For this sort of conversation another 'walkie-talkie' word is used:

baat   chiit   conversation, discussion
matter nonsense word

EXERCISES

1

Any questions

On this radio chat show interviewer Asif Hussain asks Kamla Bharati some questions, but they're in the wrong order. Renumber them to fit Kamla's answers.

Asif

a **achchhaa, kyaa aapko mirch-masaalaa pasand hai?**

b **aapko angrezii khaanaa kaisaa lagtaa hai?**

c **aapko kis Kism kaa khaanaa pasand hai?**

d **kyaa aap gosht nahĩĩ khaatĩĩ?**

Kamla

1 **mujhe sabzii pasand hai.**

2 **jii nahĩĩ, gosht mujhe bahut buraa lagtaa hai.**

3 **buraa to nahĩĩ lagtaa, magar achchhaa bhii nahĩĩ lagtaa.**

4 **jii hãã, bahut pasand hai.**

2

Any answers

This interviewee's hobby is reading and she especially likes reading Urdu books. She has also been learning Hindi for the past two years, and likes it very much. How does she answer the interviewer's questions?

Interviewer

a **aapke kyaa kyaa shauK hãĩ?** _____

b **achchhaa, aapko kis Kism kii kitaabẽ pasand hãĩ?** _____

c **kyaa aapkaa koii aur bhii shauK hai?** _____

d **kab se siikh rahii hãĩ?** _____

e **aapko kaisii lagtii hai?** _____

3

Pastimes

Here are several people describing their favourite hobbies or interests. Some say **mujhe pasand hai** ('I like it'), and some say **mujhe shauK hai** ('It is my hobby'). Fill in the gaps following the example, remembering to use the right **-naa** form.

a **mujhe giTaar bajaanaa pasand hai.**

b **mujhe _____ kaa shauK hai.**

c **mujhe _____ kaa shauK hai.**

d **mujhe sangiit _____ pasand hai.**

e **mujhe _____ pasand hai.**

f **mujhe** cricket **_____ pasand hai.**

g **mujhe** French **_____ kaa shauK hai.**

h **mujhe filmē _____ kaa shauK hai.**

4
What what?

Key question words are missing from this conversation. Fill the blanks with **kyaa, kyaa kyaa, kaun, kaun kaun, kahãa,** or **kahãa kahãa.**

Abdul Malik:	aapkaa naam _____ hai?
Harinder Singh:	Harinder Singh.
Abdul Malik:	aap _____ rahte hãi?
Harinder Singh:	Cornwall Rd. **par.**
Abdul Malik:	vahãa aur _____ rahte hãi?
Harinder Singh:	**mere pitaajii hãi, merii maataajii hãi, aur meraa choTaa bhaaii bhii hai.**
Abdul Malik:	aapke pitaajii kaa naam _____ hai?
Harinder Singh:	**sardaar gurbachan singh.**
Abdul Malik:	_____ aap kaam karte hãi?
Harinder Singh:	**jii hãa, bahut kaam kartaa hũu.**
Abdul Malik:	**achchhaa,** aap _____ kaam karte hãi?
Harinder Singh:	**mãi** factory **mẽ** machine operator **hũu.** Clubs **mẽ gaanaa bhii gaataa hũu. bahut kaam kartaa hũu.**
Abdul Malik:	aap _____ kaam karte hãi?
Harinder Singh:	Bradford **mẽ, aur** Huddersfield **mẽ.**
Abdul Malik:	**aapke saath aur** _____ **gaataa hai?**
Harinder Singh:	**meraa chhoTaa bhaaii.**

5
achchhaa buraa

Following the examples say whether you like or dislike these foods and drinks. You will need to remember – or look up! – the genders.

a   **mujhe pulaav achchhaa lagtaa hai**

b   **mujhe sharaab burii lagtii hai**

c   **mujhe** _____ _____ _____

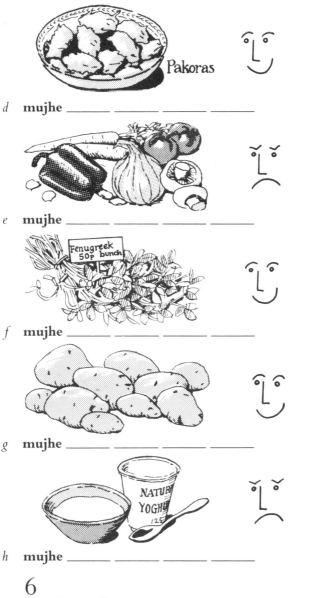

d   **mujhe** _____ _____ _____

e   **mujhe** _____ _____ _____

f   **mujhe** _____ _____ _____

g   **mujhe** _____ _____ _____

h   **mujhe** _____ _____ _____

6
kyaa/kaun/kis

Two friends are having a row about the food they're eating. Fill in
the blanks with **kyaa**, **kaun**, or **kis**.

Satpal	Kalyan
ye _____ **hai?**	**ye tumhaaraa khaanaa hai.**
khaanaa? ye _____ **Kism kaa**	
khaanaa hai?	**ye pulaav hai.**

mujhe pasand nahĩĩ hai. vo
_____ kii pleT hai?   ye? ye merii pleT hai.
usmẽ _____ hai?   ismẽ bhii pulaav hai.
ye khaanaa _____ ne
banaayaa?   mere dost ne.
tumhaaraa dost _____ hai?   ranjiit.
usko khaanaa banaanaa nahĩĩ
aataa.   _____ ko?
ranjiit ko.

7
Walkie-talkie

Each of the words on the outside of the circle can be paired with one
of the words on the inside. Pick a word from inside the circle to fill
the gaps in the dialogues below. (You will have to use one of them
twice.) Most of these 'nonsense word' pairs you have already come
across. You should be able to guess the new ones quite easily. What
do you think they mean? You will find rough translations in the exercise key.

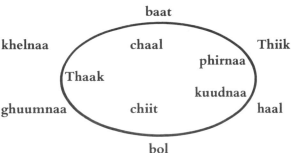

baat

khelnaa   chaal   Thiik
    phirnaa
Thaak
    kuudnaa
ghuumnaa   chiit   haal

bol

a   kyaa haal-_____ hai?
    Thiik-_____ hai.
b   aapke kyaa kyaa shauK hãĩ?
    mujhe khelnaa-_____ pasand hai. mujhe ghuumne-_____
    kaa bhii shauK hai.
c   kyaa aapko urduu yaa hindii aatii hai?
    bol-_____ kii zabaan aatii hai. baat-_____ kar saktaa hũũ
    magar likh-paRh nahĩĩ saktaa.

 # 8
Listening exercise

Ten people were asked what they thought of the latest record,
'Bhangra Bash', by the popular group, Play Punjabi. Listen to their
replies. Is it going to be a hit? How many like it?

BACKGROUND

POETRY AND LITERATURE

As we have already said, modern Hindi and Urdu are both based on the language spoken in and around Delhi. The first major writer who wrote in this dialect (known as Khari Boli) is Amir Khusro (1253–1327). The *modern* Urdu literature, however, began in the eighteenth century and *modern* Hindi literature in Khari Boli a century later. (Much older and very rich Hindi literature in other dialects such as Braj Bhasha, Avadhi, Rajasthani and Maithili also exists). Some of the best Hindi and Urdu writers – past and present – come from non-Hindi/Urdu-speaking areas, and some of the major Urdu writers have been, and are, Hindus and Sikhs.

There have been a large number of poets and prose writers both in Urdu and Hindi in the past. A few of them wrote in both the languages. Prem Chand, an eminent novelist and short story writer of this century, wrote in both Urdu and Hindi. His Hindi is said to be Urdu-like and his Urdu Hindi-like. Classical Urdu poetry dealt largely with subjects like wine (mostly as a symbol or metaphor), beauty and the various facets of love. The favourite form of poetry was ghazal. Ghalib, Dagh, the last Mughal emperor Bahadur Shah Zafar and many other poets of the nineteenth century wrote in this vein. While this trend continues, other strains have been appearing since the beginning of this century. Iqbal wrote philosophical poetry and Faiz and many other poets with Marxist leanings also dealt with social themes. Jigar, Firaq, Josh and Faraz are other prominent Urdu poets of this century. Social realism is the norm in Urdu fiction. Prem Chand, Rajinder Singh Bedi, S. H. Manto, Ismat Chughtai and Krishan Chandar are representative 'realist' writers.

Hindi poets (with one major exception) have generally ignored the traditional subjects of ghazal. Religion, culture, nature and mysticism were the favourite subjects for poets like Prasad, Pant, Nirala and Mahadevi Varma. Harivansh Rai Bachchan (father of the famous modern film star Amitabh) is best known for his *Madhushala* ('Wine Tavern') written in an Omar Khayyam style in praise of wine and with profound disrespect for religious fundamentalism. The quatrains of this book have been relished by readers and listeners for about half a century. 'Progressive' poetry under the Marxist influence has also been written. It is difficult to fit the great modern Hindi poet and novelist Agyeya into any pigeonhole. Major modern Hindi novelists and short story writers are Prem Chand, Upendra Nath Ashq, Yashpal, Agyeya and Nirmal Varma.

Poetry is very much a performance art in India and Pakistan. The English term 'poetry recital' is not an adequate translation of Urdu *mushayara* or Hindi *kavi sammelan*. In a *mushayara* or *kavi sammelan*, audience participation in the form of applause, spontaneous expressions of appreciation and requests for repetition of lines are an essential feature. So a good poet can expect to be constantly interrupted, by the audience and by the other poets sharing the stage, with interjections and expressions like *vah vah* ('well done!'), *mukarrar, phir se kahiye* ('please repeat') etc. A single line may be repeated several times, building up suspense to be resolved in the next line.

In Britain, in the sixties, a number of Urdu literary societies were established in Nottingham, Bradford, London and other places. These societies organised *mushayaras* and seminars for the general promotion and development of Urdu literature in Britain. Out of these developed Urdu Markaz ('Urdu Centre'), now based in London, which has published a number of prose and poetry books and also functions as a link between Indian and Pakistani Urdu writers and poets.

aapko kahãã jaanaa hai?

TALKING ABOUT TRAVEL

SAYING WHAT YOU ARE GOING TO DO

TIMES OF THE DAY

 1

While in Bradford Sneh went to Bharat travel agency to book a plane ticket. She spoke to Ramubhai Ahir:

Sneh:	Hello Ramubhai.
Ramubhai:	Hello **jii. kyaa haal hai?**
Sneh:	**Thiik hai. aap kaise hãĩ?**
Ramubhai:	**mãĩ bhii Thiik hũũ. mãĩ aapke liye kyaa kar saktaa hũũ?**
Sneh:	**mujhe do TikTẽ chaahiyẽ.**
Ramubhai:	**aapko kahãã jaanaa hai?**
Sneh:	**mãĩ laahaur jaanaa chaahtii hũũ.**
Ramubhai:	**aapko kab jaanaa hai?**
Sneh:	**janvarii mẽ jaanaa hai.**
Ramubhai:	**aur vaapas kab aanaa hai?**
Sneh:	**farvarii mẽ.**

NOTES

Ramubhai asks Sneh's destination:

aapko kahãã jaanaa hai?   Where do you intend to go?
you-to where to go   is   Where are you going?

She tells him where she wants to go:
mãĩ laahaur jaanaa chaahtii hũũ.
I   Lahore   to go   wanting   am

I want to go to Lahore.

Ramubhai asks her when she intends to go and come back:
aapko kab   jaanaa hai?   When do you intend to go?
you-to when to go   is   When are you going?
(aapko) vaapas kab   aanaa   hai?
(you-to) back   when to come is

When do you intend to come back?
When are you coming back?

CHECK-UP 1 When does Sneh intend to go to Lahore?

2

Meanwhile Omar was asking Daulat Singh for advice on how to travel to Srinagar in the Vale of Kashmir:

Omar:	**landan se dillii tak mãĩ havaaii jahaaz se jaaũũgaa. magar dillii se shriinagar kaise jaaũ?**
Daulat:	**agar aap havaaii jahaaz se jaaẽ to kam vaKt lagegaa.**
Omar:	**magar mãĩ havaaii jahaaz se shriinagar nahĩĩ jaanaa chaahtaa. kyaa mãĩ Tren yaa bas mẽ jaa saktaa hũũ?**
Daulat:	**mere Khayaal mẽ aap jammuu tak kaa safar Tren mẽ karẽ.**
Omar:	**Thiik hai.**
Daulat:	**aur jammuu se shriinagar bas mẽ jaaẽ.**
Omar:	**jii Thiik hai. mãĩ aise hii karũũgaa. shukriyaa.**

NOTES

Omar is clear about the trip as far as Delhi, but unsure of how to go on from there:

landan se   dillii tak   mãĩ havaaii jahaaz se
London -from Delhi -upto I   aeroplane   -from
jaaũũgaa . . .   I will go from London to Delhi
will go   by plane . . .
magar (mãĩ) dillii se   shriinagar kaise jaaũũ?
but   (I)   Delhi -from Srinagar   how   may go
                              . . . but how may I go from Delhi
                              to Srinagar?

Daulat Singh advises him:
agar aap havaaii jahaaz se   jaaẽ   to   kam vaKt
if   you   aeroplane -from should go then less   time
lagegaa   If you go by plane, it will take
will strike   less time.

Omar isn't keen:
magar mãĩ havaaii jahaaz se   nahĩĩ jaanaa chaahtaa
but   I   aeroplane   -from not to go   wanting
                              But I don't want to go by plane.
kyaa mãĩ Tren yaa bas mẽ jaa saktaa hũũ?
(Q)   I   train or bus -in go   can
                              Can I go by train or bus?

Daulat Singh suggests an alternative:
mere Khayaal mẽ . . . aap jammuu tak   kaa safar
my   opinion -in   you Jammu -upto -of journey
Tren mẽ karẽ . . .   I think that you should travel as
train -in may do   far as Jammu by train . . .
aur (aap) jammuu se   shriinagar bas mẽ jaaẽ
and (you) Jammu -from Srinagar   bus -in may go
                              . . . and go from Jammu to
                              Srinagar by bus.

Omar is convinced:
mãĩ aise hii   karũũgaa   I will do exactly that.
I   thus only will do

CHECK-UP 2 How does Omar decide to travel from Delhi to Jammu/Jammu to Srinagar?

3

Business completed, Omar and Sneh plan the next day's activities:

Omar: **to** Sneh **jii, kal kaa kyaa programm hai?**

Sneh: **kal subah hamẽ yahãã kaa** photographic museum **dekhnaa hai.
aur kuchh kitaabẽ bhii Khariidnii hãĩ.**

Omar: **aur dopahar kaa khaanaa kahãã khaaẽge?**

Sneh: Taj Restaurant **mẽ?**

Omar: **agar vahãã khaanaa khaanaa hai to pahle** booking **karnii
hogii.**

Sneh: **Thiik hai. kar lẽge.**

Omar: **hãã, yaad rahe, shaam ko hamẽ** cinema **bhii jaanaa hai.**

Sneh: **achchhaa, Thiik hai.**

NOTES

Omar asks what's planned:

kal kaa kyaa programm hai?
tomorrow -of what programme is

> What's tomorrow's programme?

Sneh tells him what's happening in the morning:

kal subah hamẽ ... museum **dekhnaa hai** ...
tomorrow morning to us ... museum to see is ...

> Tomorrow morning we are to
> see the ... museum ...

...aur kuchh kitaabẽ bhii Khariidnii hãĩ.
and   some   books   also to buy   are

           ... and to buy some books too.

Omar is interested in lunch:

aur (ham) dopahar kaa khaanaa kahãã khaaẽge?
and (we) noon   -of food   where will eat

           And where will we have lunch?

When he hears Sneh's suggestion he gives a warning:

agar (hamẽ) vahãã khaanaa khaanaa hai to   pahle
if   (to us) there meal   to eat   is then first
booking **karnii hogii**   If we are eating there, then we'll
booking to do   will be   have to book first.

Sneh agrees:

Thiik hai. (ham) kar lẽge.   Okay. We will.
fine is (we)   do will 'take'

Omar adds a reminder for the evening:

yaad   rahe...   Remember...
memory should stay
shaam ko hamẽ cinema **bhii jaanaa hai**
evening -to to us cinema also to go   is

           ... in the evening, we are to
           go to the cinema as well.

CHECK-UP 3 Where will Sneh and Omar have lunch?

KEYWORDS

△ **TikaT** (f)	ticket
△ **TikTẽ** (f)	tickets
△ **laahaur**	Lahore
△ **chaah**	want
△ **janvarii** (m)	January
△ **vaapas aa**	come back
△ **farvarii** (m)	February
△ **landan**	London
△ **dillii**	Delhi
△ **tak**	up to/as far as
△ **havaaii jahaaz** (m)	aeroplane
△ **mãĩ . . . jaaũũgaa**	I (masc.) will go . . .
△ **shriinagar**	Srinagar
△ **mãĩ . . . jaaũũ**	I may go . . .
△ **aap . . . jaaẽ**	you may go . . .
△ **Khayaal** (m)	opinion
△ **safar** (m)	journey
△ **safar kar**	travel (verb)
△ **aap . . . safar karẽ**	you may travel . . .
△ **jammuu**	Jammu
△ **mãĩ . . . karũũgaa**	I (masc.) will do . . .
△ **aise**	thus
△ **prograam** (m)	plan/programme
△ **kal**	tomorrow
△ **subah** (f)	morning
△ **Khariid**	buy
△ **dopahar** (m)	afternoon
△ **agar . . . to . . .**	If . . . then . . .
△ **pahle**	first
△ booking **kar**	book (verb)
△ **ho**	be/happen
△ **hamẽ** booking **karnii hogii**	we will have to book
△ **yaad** (f)	memory
△ **yaad rahe**	remember!
△ **shaam** (f)	evening
△ **parsõ**	day after tomorrow/day before yesterday
△ **narsõ**	two days after tomorrow/before yesterday
△ **mujhe afsos hai**	I'm sorry
△ **raat** (f)	night

SOUND SYSTEMS

Kh AND G

As with **k** and **K** (see Unit 8 Sound Systems) some speakers make a distinction between **kh** and **Kh**, and some don't. **Kh** is exactly like the 'ch' sound in the Scottish word 'loch'. It is pronounced in the same part of the mouth as **k** and **kh**, but with the tongue not quite closing with the roof of the mouth so that the air continues to escape. It is found in words borrowed from Persian and Arabic, and so you may find Urdu speakers are more conscious of it than Hindi speakers, who may replace it with **kh**. **G** (as in **Gazal**) is like **Kh** except that your vocal cords continue to vibrate while you make it. Again it occurs only in words borrowed from Persian or Arabic, and you will often hear it replaced by **g**.

HOW THE LANGUAGE WORKS

THINKING AHEAD – ANOTHER -naa FORM

In the previous unit we came across the 'seeing is believing' **-naa** form – the form that can turn verbs into masculine nouns so you can talk *about* them. Remember how Savita and Dahyanti talked about *playing* the guitar and *playing* badminton: **mujhe giTaar** *bajaane* **kaa shauK hai, mujhe** badminton *khelnaa* **pasand hai.** Now in this unit you've met a different sort of **-naa** form, to use when you're *thinking ahead*, talking about plans and obligations.

So, when Sneh and Ramubhai are planning her trip, he asks her when she is intending to go – **aapko kab** *jaanaa* **hai?** And when Sneh and Omar are planning their sightseeing day in Bradford she reminds him they have to buy some books too – **kuchh kitaabẽ bhii** *Khariidnii* **hãĩ**.

You will have spotted that **Khariidnii**, ending in **-ii** doesn't look very masculine. You're right, it isn't. That's because this 'thinking ahead' **-naa** form isn't really a noun at all and has different masculine and feminine, and singular and plural endings just like the **-taa** and **-aa** forms:

	masculine	feminine
singular	**-naa**	**-nii**
plural	**-ne**	**-nĩĩ***

* **-nĩĩ** becomes **-nii** when it is followed by **hãĩ** or **thĩĩ**.

The rules for choosing which one of these endings to use are like the rules for the **-aa** form (Unit 6), though not so complicated. The 'thinking ahead' **-naa** form, rather like the **-aa** form, agrees with its

direct object, not with what would be the 'subject' in the equivalent English sentence. So, when Sneh plans to buy *books* she says **Khariid***nii* **hãĩ** because 'books' (**kitaabẽ**) are *feminine plural*, but when she plans to see the *museum* she says **dekh***naa hai* because 'museum' is *masculine singular*.

If there is *no* direct object then the **-naa** form just stays in the masculine singular. So, when Sneh answers Ramubhai's question by saying she intends to go in January she says (**mujhe**) **janvarii mẽ jaanaa hai**, using the *masculine* singular form.

Unlike the **-aa** form, the 'subject' – in this case the person doing the planning – is not marked with the 'special agent' **-ne** (at least not in *standard* Hindi and Urdu). Instead it is marked by **ko** or one of the special 'dative' forms (like **mujhe, use** etc.) which are listed in the grammatical summary. You will probably find though that many people in Britain, particularly Punjabi speakers, *do* use **-ne** in everyday speech. But **aapne kab jaanaa hai?** (instead of **aapko kab jaanaa hai?**) is not strictly correct Hindi or Urdu.

EXPRESS DESIRE

To express simple desire (as opposed to an obligation or intention) you can use the verb **chaah** with a **-naa** form. So to say she *wants to go* to Lahore Sneh says **mãĩ laahaur** *jaanaa* **chaahtii hũũ**. This is the 'seeing is believing' **-naa** form again – a straightforward masculine noun which doesn't agree with anything. **hũũ** and **chaahtii** of course agree with the feminine singular subject **mãĩ** (in this case Sneh).

'PERSONAL POTENTIAL'

You may have noticed that up until this unit you have only met one verb form that changes according to whether the subject is 'I' or 'you' or 'he' etc. (what linguists call 'person') and that's the one you learned in the first unit – **hũũ, hai, hãĩ** etc. The **-aa, -taa**, and 'thinking ahead' **-naa** forms are like *adjectives* – they change for masculine and feminine, and singular and plural, but not for 'person'. But there *is* a special 'personal' form for every verb, which we've come across for the first time in this unit. It conveys the idea of a *potential* action or event. ('Subjunctive' is the grammatical term for it, but if you don't find that helpful to remember just think of your own '*personal potential*'.)

Remember how Omar asks about going to Srinagar: (**mãĩ**) **shriinagar kaise jaaũũ?** This can be roughly translated as 'How should I go to Srinagar?' or 'How can I go to Srinagar?' or even 'How may I go to Srinagar?'. The essential point is that the 'going' is seen as

potential rather than *actual* or *definite*. And, when Daulat Singh advises him, he suggests *potential* rather than *definite* courses of action: **mere Khayaal mẽ aap jammuu tak kaa safar Tren mẽ *karẽ* aur jammuu se shriinagar bas mẽ *jaaẽ*** – 'I think you *should* travel as far as Jammu by train, and *should* go from Jammu to Srinagar by bus.'

The 'personal potential' or 'subjunctive' endings are perfectly regular and very easy to learn. All you have to do is add them to the verb stem. Here are all the different endings, using **jaa** as an example:

mãĩ jaa*ũũ*
tuu jaa*e*
ye/vo (sg.) **jaa*e***
ham jaa*ẽ*
tum jaa*o*
ye/vo (pl.) **aap jaa*ẽ***

The one very important exception is of course with **hũũ, hai, hãĩ** etc., which, as you know, are 'personal' forms already. Since **hai** does not have any special *potential* ('may be') forms, we have to use another verb **ho** ('happen/become') in its place, whose *potential* forms are as follows:

mãĩ hũũ
tuu ho
ye/vo (sg.) **ho**
ham hõ
tum ho
ye/vo (pl.) **aap hõ**

'DEFINITE POTENTIAL' – THE HINDI AND URDU -gaa FORM

In Hindi and Urdu there is a very simple way of changing 'may' into 'will', of making something *potential* into something *definite*. All you have to do is add a special 'definite' **-gaa** form to the 'personal potential' verb. Remember how Omar decides on a definite course of action after talking with Daulat Singh: **mãĩ aise hii karũũgaa** – 'I will do exactly that'. 'May do' **(karũũ)** becomes 'will do' just by adding 'definite' **-gaa**. If you think of the future as *definite potential* you can easily see the sense of it. Remember also Daulat Singh's advice on flying: **agar aap havaaii jahaaz se *jaaẽ* to kam vaKt lagegaa**. It is clear that the journey will *definitely* take less time *should* Omar go by plane.

As you might expect, the **-gaa** form, like the **-taa** form and others, has the usual adjectival endings:

	masculine	feminine
singular	**-gaa**	**-gii**
plural	**-ge**	**-gii***

* There is no **-gĩĩ** form.

They agree with the same thing that the 'potential' form agrees with. When Omar asks Sneh where they will have lunch he says **(ham) dopahar kaa khaanaa kahãã khaaẽge? -ge** here is masculine plural to agree with the implicit **ham** (Omar and Sneh). **khaaẽ** also agrees with the **ham**.

To express *future obligation* the **-gaa** form can be combined with the 'thinking ahead' **-naa** form: **pahle hamẽ** booking **karnii hogii** – 'We'll have to book first'. Here the **-naa** form agrees with its *direct object* 'booking' (feminine singular) as you would expect, and **ho** and **gii** likewise follow suit.

AWAYDAYS

In Hindi and Urdu, **kal** may mean either 'yesterday' or 'tomorrow'. **parsõ** is either 'the day before yesterday' or 'the day after tomorrow', and **narsõ** 'the day before the day before yesterday' or 'the day after the day after tomorrow'. So choosing the right verb form becomes quite important in order to distinguish past from future!

EXERCISES

1

Connections

You're planning a trip around the subcontinent. Your travel agent advises you on how to go from place to place. But how good is her advice? Check the information she gives you against this chart. Put a tick or a cross in each box to show whether the advice she gives is right or wrong.

Key: b = bus
p = plane
t = train
n = no direct connection

	Mirpur	Islamabad	Delhi	Agra	Calcutta	Dhaka	Sylhet	Colombo
Mirpur								
Islamabad	b							
Delhi	n	p						
Agra	n	n	bpt					
Calcutta	n	p	pt	p				
Dhaka	n	p	p	n	p			
Sylhet	n	n	n	n	n	b		
Colombo	n	p	p	n	p	p	n	

You: **islaamaabaad se miirpur tak kaise jaa saktaa hū̃?**

Travel agent: **agar aap havaaii jahaaz se jaaē̃ to kam vaKt lagegaa.** ☐ *a*

You: **Thiik hai. mãı̃ aise hii karū̃ugaa. aur miirpur se mãı̃ dillii jaanaa chaahtaa hū̃.**

Travel agent: **pahle aapko islaamaabaad vaapas jaanaa hogaa. vahā̃ se aap havaaii jahaaz le sakte hãı̃.** ☐ *b*

You: **achchhaa. aur dillii se mujhe aagraa jaanaa hai. kaise jaa saktaa hū̃?**

Travel agent: **dillii se aagraa tak aap Tren yaa bas yaa havaaii jahaaz le sakte hãı̃.** ☐ *c*

You: **aagraa se Dhaakaa tak kyaa mãı̃ bas mẽ jaa saktaa hū̃?**

Travel agent: **jii nahī̃. pahle aapko kalkattaa jaanaa hogaa.** ☐ *d*

You: **kyaa mãı̃ kalkattaa tak bas mẽ jaa saktaa hū̃?**

Travel agent: **jii hā̃.** ☐ *e*

You: **aur kalkattaa se Dhaakaa tak kaise jaaū̃?**

Travel agent: **mere Khayaal mẽ aap Tren mẽ jaaē̃.** ☐ *f*

You:	**Thiik hai. aur vahãã se silhaT tak?**
Travel agent:	**Dhaakaa se silhaT tak aap havaaii jahaaz se jaa sakte hãĩ.** ☐ *g*
You:	**aur silhaT se kalambo tak kaise jaa saktaa hũũ?**
Travel agent:	**pahle aapko Dhaakaa vaapas jaanaa hogaa. vahãã se aap havaaii jahaaz se jaa sakte hãĩ.** ☐ *h*

 ## 2
Neighbours

A friend who lives nearby in Glasgow calls to say he's going away for a few days and would like you to keep an eye on his house while he's gone. You have to find out when he's going and coming back, and you're a little curious about the trip anyway.

a   First you ask him where he intends to go – **aapko kahãã jaanaa hai?**

b   He says **mujhe** Edinburgh **jaanaa hai**. Now ask him when he intends to go.

c   His answer is **mujhe aaj jaanaa hai**. Ask him when he's coming back.

d   He says **mujhe** Edinburgh **se vaapas nahĩĩ aanaa. vahãã se mujhe** Dundee **jaanaa hai**. Ask him when he's going there.

e   He answers **mujhe kal subah vahãã jaanaa hai**. Ask him how he intends to go there – by bus or by train?

f   He says **mujhe Tren mẽ jaanaa hai**. Ask him when he's going to get back from Dundee.

g   He says **maaluum nahĩĩ**. Tell him you're sorry (**mujhe afsos hai**), but tomorrow you're going to London, by plane.

3
Shopping list

These are the items on your shopping list. Make a sentence for each one following the example given. Be careful to make the **-naa** form of **Khariid** agree with the object.

a   **mujhe sabziyãã Khariidnii hãĩ**

b   _____

c   _____

e _____

d _____

f _____

g _____

4
Planning the week

You're planning your activities for the week. The ones you've marked with a question mark are things you *want* to do, but they're not yet definite. Tell a friend what you're planning following the examples. (The days of the week in Hindi and Urdu are given in the word lists at the end of the book, though you'll find people often use the English names.)

	MORNING	AFTERNOON	EVENING
Mon	Write to Rajiv?	Lunch at Anarkali Restaurant	Hindi Class
Tues	◄————LONDON———————►	(Buy some Hindi books?)	
Wed			Badminton?
Thur	◄————BRISTOL?————►		
Fri	Swimming?		Cinema

e.g. Monday **ko mujhe hindii siikhnii hai**
Wednesday **ko maĩ** badminton **khelnaa chaahtii/chaahtaa hũũ.**

5
So what?

agar aap havaaii jahaaz se jaaẽ to kam vaKt lagegaa – if you go by plane it takes less time. Here are some more **agar . . . to . . .** sentences. Supply the appropriate form of the verb in brackets.

a **agar maĩ urduu (siikh) to paakistaanii dostõ ke saath baat-chiit kar (sak).**

b **agar aap khaanaa (banaa) to ham khaa (le).**

c **agar aap merii kaar Thiik kar (de) to mā̃i aapko 50** pound **de (de).**

d **agar aap angrezii siikhnaa (chaah) to mā̃i aapko sikhaa (de).**

e **agar aap ye khaanaa (khaa) to aapke peT mē dard (ho).**

f **agar aap ismē thoRaa dhaniyaa (Daal) to ye pulaav aur bhii achchhaa (lag).**

g **agar mā̃i gaanaa (gaa) to mujhe kaun (sun)?**

h **agar mā̃i giTaar (bajaa) to merii beTii gaanaa (gaa).**

i **agar aap hindii mē (bol) to ye samajh (le).**

j **agar aap hindii mē chiTThii (likh) to mujhe bahut achchhaa (lag).**

6
Time travel

The day in Hindi and Urdu can be divided roughly as follows:

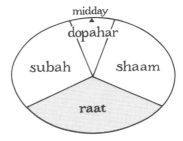

These people are all planning trips tomorrow. What time of day do they say they will travel? Use the train timetable on the next page to make a sentence for each on the pattern of the example given. Remember to use the right **-gaa** form.

a **kal dopahar ham** Birmingham **jaaē̃ge.**

b _____
_____

c _____

d _____

e _____

f _____

Dep. Time	Destination
0830	London
1203	Birmingham
1321	Bristol
1644	Derby
1826	Plymouth
2314	Glasgow

7
Yesterday and tomorrow

The word **kal** in Hindi and Urdu can mean either yesterday or tomorrow. The context tells you which. Look at the verb endings in these sentences and decide if they are about yesterday or tomorrow.

a **kal mãĩne bahut achchhaa khaanaa khaayaa.** yesterday/tomorrow

b **kal mãĩ** London **gayaa thaa.** yesterday/tomorrow

c **kal mujhe** Edinburgh **jaanaa hai.** yesterday/tomorrow

d **kal mãĩ bahut kaam karũũgaa.** yesterday/tomorrow

e **kal mãĩ fuTbaal khelnaa chaahtaa hũũ.** yesterday/tomorrow

f **kal mãĩne kuchh hindii kii kitaabẽ Khariidĩĩ.** yesterday/tomorrow

g **kal mujhe ek urduu kii kitaab Khariidnii hai.** yesterday/tomorrow

 # 8
Listening exercise

Listen to these people talking about their travel plans. Note down as much information as you can about when, where, and how they're going.

BACKGROUND

URDU AND HINDI CALLIGRAPHY

The traditions of calligraphy in the scripts used for writing both Urdu (Perso-Arabic) and Hindi (Devanagari) are of great antiquity. It is, however, only in the Perso-Arabic tradition that calligraphy has attained a very high status as a fine art very often cultivated for its own sake. With the invention of printing, the tradition of calligraphy in the scripts indigenous to India declined. But the Perso-Arabic tradition flourishes even today. Metallic type for printing in the Arabic script was first prepared in the eighteenth century, and now many sophisticated wordprocessing systems are also available. But still, most printing in the major stylistic varieties of the Arabic script is done from handwritten sheets.

There are two major styles of the Arabic script. The original Arabic style is called *Naskh* (pronounced **nasKh**), and the style used for writing Urdu, Persian and some other languages is called *Nastaliq* (pronounced as **nastaaliiK**) or the Perso-Arabic style. Verses from the Koran (the Muslim holy book), even when they are quoted in an Urdu text, are written in Naskh. The Urdu type used for printing and on typewriters is Naskh-based. However, the differences between

The Taj Mahal.

the two styles are minor and relate to the shapes of the letters only. You can easily read Naskh writing once you have mastered Nastaliq. (The Nastaliq script here says 'Daily Jang, London welcomes Hindi Urdu Bol Chaal programme.')

Nastaliq calligraphy

روزنامہ جنگ لندن ہندی
اردو بول چال پروگرام کا
خیر مقدم کرتا ہے

Nastaliq has been used to great artistic effect in manuscripts, paintings and symbolic drawings (writing a secular verse in such a way that its meaning is also represented by the figure – human, animal or whatever – the drawing as a whole creates or suggests). A greater artistic glory has been achieved by Naskh calligraphy in manuscripts, paintings and on walls and domes in mosques and mausoleums like the Taj Mahal.

aur uske baad?

1

In their conversation Sneh first of all asked Rizwana Firdous about where she was born and when she came to Britain:

Sneh: Rizwana **(rizvaanaa), aap kahã̄ paidaa huii thĩ̄?**
Rizwana: **mã̄i kashmiir mẽ paidaa huii, magar jab mã̄i chhoTii thii, tab mã̄i apne vaalid, vaalidaa, aur bhaaii ke saath yahã̄ aa gaii.**
Sneh: **jab aap is mulk mẽ aãĩ, tab aapkii umr kitnii thii?**
Rizwana: **us vaKt merii umr chhe saal kii thii.**

NOTES

Sneh's first question was about Rizwana's birthplace:

aap kahãã paidaa huii   thĩĩ?
you where born   happened were

           Where were you born?

After saying she was born in Kashmir (**mãĩ kashmiir mẽ paidaa huii**), Rizwana added that she came here (with her family) when she was small:

magar jab   mãĩ chhoTii thii, tab mãĩ... yahãã aa   gaii
but   when I   small   was, then I   here   come gone

           But I came here when I was
           small.

Sneh asked how old she was:

jab   aap is mulk mẽ aaĩ, tab aapkii umr kitnii   thii?
when you this country -in came, then your   age how much was

           How old were you when you
           came to this country?

Rizwana replied that she was six:

us   vaKt merii umr chhe saal kii thii
that time my   age six   years -of was

           I was six years old at the time.

CHECK-UP 1 Who came to Britain with Rizwana?

2

They then went on to talk about school and higher education:

Sneh: **to aapkii paRhaaii yahãã huii?**
Rizwana: **jii hãã, sab se pahle** Gorbals Primary **mẽ, aur uske baad** Adelphi Secondary **mẽ.**
Sneh: **skuul ke baad aapne kyaa kiyaa?**
Rizwana: **skuul ke baad mãĩne** teacher training **kii. aur tab se aaj tak mãĩ kaii kaam kar chukii hũũ.**

NOTES

Sneh asked if Rizwana was educated here:

to aapkii paRhaaii yahãã huii?
so your   education here   happened

           So you were educated here?

Rizwana told her the names of the schools:

jii hãã, sab se   pahle Gorbals Primary **mẽ,**
yes,   all-from first   Gorbals Primary -in

           Yes, first of all in Gorbals
           Primary...

aur uske baad Adelphi Secondary **mē.**
and that-of after Adelphi Secondary -in

> . . . and after that in Adelphi
> Secondary.

Sneh asked what Rizwana did after leaving school (**skuul ke baad aapne kyaa kiyaa?**). Rizwana told her that she did teacher training and that since then she had done many sorts of work:

tab se aaj tak mãi kaii kaam kar chukii hũu.
then-from today-till I several jobs do finished am

> Since then I've done many jobs.

CHECK-UP 2 Where was Rizwana educated?

 3

They then talked about the jobs Rizwana had done:

Sneh:	**aapne kyaa kyaa kaam kiye hãi?**
Rizwana:	**sab se pahle mãine** primary school teacher **kaa kaam kiyaa. uske baad mãi** community link teacher **ban gaii. phir mãine** youth leader **kaa kaam kiyaa, aur** women's refuge **mē bhii kaam kiyaa.**
Sneh:	Women's refuge **mē aapne kyaa kaam kiyaa?**
Rizwana:	**vahãa mãi angrezii paRhaa rahii thii.**
Sneh:	**rizvaanaa, vahãa kaun-kaun sii zabaanē bolii jaatii thĩi?**
Rizwana:	**angrezii ke saath-saath urduu, panjaabii, aur hindii.**
Sneh:	**to aapko chaar zabaanē aatii hãi?**
Rizwana:	**jii hãã.**

NOTES

When Sneh asked her what jobs she'd done in the past (**aapne kyaa kyaa kaam kiye hãi?**), Rizwana listed them in order:

sab se pahle mãine primary school teacher **kaa kaam kiyaa.**
all-from first I   primary school teacher -of work done

> First of all I worked as a primary
> school teacher.

uske baad mãi community link teacher **ban gaii.**
that-of after I community link teacher become gone

> After that I became a community
> link teacher.

phir mãine youth leader **kaa kaam kiyaa**
then I   youth leader -of work done

> Then I worked as a youth leader . . .

aur women's refuge **mē bhii kaam kiyaa.**
and women's refuge -in also work done

> . . . and I also worked in a
> women's refuge.

Sneh also asked about the languages spoken in the women's refuge:
vahãã kaun-kaun sii zabaanẽ bolii   jaatii thĩĩ?
there   which-which   languages spoken going were
                                    Which languages were spoken
                                    there?

Rizwana told her which languages were used alongside English:
angrezii ke saath-saath urduu, panjaabii, aur hindii
English   -of alongside   Urdu,   Punjabi,   and Hindi
                                    Urdu, Punjabi, and Hindi
                                    alongside English.

CHECK-UP 3 What was Rizwana's second job?

4
Sneh and Omar put some similar questions to stockbroker, Naseer
Dean, and the editor of the *Daily Jang*, Mr Kazi:

Sneh:	**aap kahãã paidaa hue?**
Naseer:	**mãĩ yahãã** London **mẽ paidaa huaa. mere daadaa jaan** 1920's **mẽ yahãã aae the.**
Sneh:	**yahãã unhõne kyaa kaam kiyaa?**
Naseer:	**vo** sports business **mẽ the. yahãã aakar unhõne** cricket bats, squash rackets **vaGairaa bechne kaa kaam shuruu kiyaa.**
Omar:	**yahãã aakar aapne kyaa kiyaa?**
Mr Kazi:	**yahãã aakar mãĩne** engineering **mẽ** degree **lii.**
Omar:	**phir?**
Mr Kazi:	**phir paakistaan vaapas jaakar apnaa kaarobaar kiyaa.**

Notes

Naseer explained that his grandfather (**daadaa jaan**) started a business selling sports equipment after coming to Britain:

yahãã aakar		**unhône** bats...	**vaGairaa bechne kaa kaam**
here	having come he	bats... etc.	selling -of work
shuruu kiyaa			After coming here he started a
start	done		business selling bats etc.

Omar asked Mr Kazi what he did after coming to Britain (**yahãã aakar aapne kyaa kiyaa?**):

yahãã aakar	**mãĩne** engineering **mẽ** degree **lii.**
here having come I	engineering -in degree taken
	After coming here I took a
	degree in engineering.
phir paakistaan vaapas	**jaakar**	**apnaa kaarobaar**
then Pakistan back	having gone my business
kiyaa	Then, after going back to
done	Pakistan, I ran my own business.

CHECK-UP 4 Did Mr Kazi get his engineering degree before or after coming to Britain?

KEYWORDS

△	**paidaa**	born
△	**paidaa ho**	be born
△	**aap . . . paidaa huii thĩĩ**	you were born . . .
△	**jab . . . tab . . .**	when . . . then . . .
△	**aa gaii**	came
△	**mulk** (m)	country (Urdu)
△	**umr** (f)	age
△	**chhe**	six
△	**saal** (m)	year
△	**huii/huaa/hue**	happened (**ho** + **-aa**)
△	**sab**	all
△	**sab se pahle**	first of all
△	**ke baad**	after
△	**uske baad**	after that
△	**kiyaa/kii/kiye**	done (**-aa** form of **kar**)
△	**kaii**	several
△	**chuk**	complete (verb)
△	**kar chukii/chukaa hũũ**	(I) have done (and finished) (see 'How the Language Works')
△	**ban**	become
△	**ban gaii**	became
△	**phir**	then
△	**paRhaa**	teach
△	**bolii jaatii thĩĩ**	were spoken
△	**ke saath-saath**	along with
△	**daadaa jaan** (m)	grandfather (paternal)
△	**aakar**	having come
△	**vaGairaa**	etcetera
△	**bech**	sell
△	**shuruu kar**	begin, start
△	**vaapas jaakar**	having gone back
△	**kaarobaar** (m)	business
△	**jahãã**	where
△	**jo**	which (direct)
△	**jis**	which (oblique)
△	**jaisaa**	as
△	**vaisaa**	such
△	**jitnaa**	as much
△	**utnaa**	so much
△	**raah** (f)	way/path

△	**bhar**	pay
△	**desh** (m)	country (Hindi)
△	**vesh** (m)	dress
△	**chaay** (f)	tea
△	**aThaaraa**	eighteen
△	**pãach**	five
△	**Gazal** (f)	ghazal
△	**sitaar** (m)	sitar

SOUND SYSTEMS

f and ph, z and j

Like **K, Kh,** and **G, f** and **z** occur only in words borrowed from other languages, like Persian, Arabic, and also English. They don't cause any problems for speakers of English when you say them, as the same sounds occur in English too. However, you may find when you are listening to speakers of Hindi and Urdu that some people don't use **f** and **z**, but instead use **ph** and **j**. So you may hear **jahaaj** rather than **jahaaz**, or **phuTbaal** instead of **fuTbaal**. Such pronunciations, although common, may be frowned upon. The situation is slightly further confused by the fact that people who do use **f** and **z** may sometimes 'over-use' them. You will often hear **phir** pronounced as **fir**, for example.

HOW THE LANGUAGE WORKS

SAY WHEN

You already know how to *ask* 'when' in Hindi and Urdu. Remember from Unit 7 how Sneh asked Fahmeeda how long ('since when') she'd been learning German: **aap German kab se siikh rahii hãi?**

But **kab** is a *question* word – you can't use it to *say* 'when'. For that you need a *different* (though related) word – **jab. jab** is 'relative' – you use it to *relate* one thing to another *in time*. So, when Rizwana says she came to this country *when she was small* she uses **jab**, not **kab:** *jab mãi chhoTii thii*, tab mãi yahãa aa gaii* – more literally 'When I was small, then I came here'. And when Sneh asks her how old she was *when she came* she also uses **jab:** *jab aap is mulk mẽ aaĩ*, tab aapkii umr kitnii thii?* (Don't get confused by the fact that Sneh is asking a question. She's asking *how old* Rizwana was, not *when* she came.)

tab ('then') is a useful word to use with **jab**. It's not strictly necessary, but it helps to show the *relationship* between the two parts of the sentence, so learn **jab** and **tab** as a 'relative' pair. Above all, remember

that, while in English you can *say* when and you can *ask* when, in Hindi and Urdu you say **jab** but ask **kab**.

Like **jab, tab** and **kab** there are other similar 'relative' pairs and related question words in Hindi and Urdu. You'll see that they're easy to learn because the question always begins with **k** and the 'relative' with **j**.

jab...	**tab**...	**kab?**
when	then	when?
jahãã...	**vahãã**...	**kahãã?**
where	there	where?
jo...	**vo** (or **so**)...	**kaun?/kyaa?** (Direct)
jis...	**us**...	**kis?** (Oblique)
who/which	he/she/it	who?/what?
jaisaa...	**vaisaa**...	**kaisaa?**
as...	such	how?
jitnaa...	**utnaa**...	**kitnaa?**
as much...	so much...	how much?

Here are some examples of the use of the 'relative' pairs in common sayings:

jahãã	**chaah**	**vahãã**	**raah**	Where there is a will there is a
where	will	there	way	way.

jo	**karegaa**	**vo/so**	**bharegaa**	Whoever commits a sin shall
who	will do	he	will pay	have to suffer for it.

jaisaa	**desh**	**vaisaa**	**vesh**	When in Rome do as the Romans
as	country	such	dress	do.

FIRST HELPING jaa – 'COMPLETE'

We first came across 'helping verbs' in Unit 7. Remember **de** and **le**, whose original meanings are 'give' and 'take' but which, as helping verbs, give the sense of 'doing for someone else' and 'doing for oneself'. **jaa** ('go') is also frequently used as a 'helping' verb. When **jaa** combines with the *stem form* of the main verb it adds a sense of *completeness* to that verb. When Rizwana says **tab mãĩ yahãã** *aa gaii* – 'then I *came* here' – the sense is that she came and settled here. When she says **uske baad mãĩ** community link teacher *ban gaii* – 'After that I *became* a community link teacher' – the sense is that she completed a whole process (of training etc).

These two examples show the use of **jaa** in its (irregular) **-aa** form – feminine singular **gaii** to agree with the subject **mãĩ** (Rizwana). But

you can also use it in the same sense in its **-taa** or **-gaa** forms. For example:

ye kaam aaj   hii   ho   jaaegaa
this work   today   only   happen 'will go'

> This work will be completed today.

jaaegaa agrees with masculine singular **kaam** and the sense it conveys is that the work will be *fully* done to everybody's satisfaction.

SECOND HELPING jaa – 'PASSIVE'

jaa as a 'helping' verb has another very important use in Hindi and Urdu, when it combines with the **-aa** form of the main verb (not with the *stem form* as in 'first helping' **jaa**). Remember how Sneh asked which languages *were spoken* at the refuge: **vahā̃ kaun-kaun sii zabaanē** *bolii jaatii thī̃?* This is like an English 'passive' sentence – the focus is on the languages being spoken, not on the people speaking them. **zabaanē** (feminine plural) is the subject of the sentence, and that's what the **-aa** form of the main verb **bol** agrees with and what the **-taa** form of the 'helping' **jaa** agrees with too.

Here are some more examples: **dhansak mē namak bhii Daalaa jaataa hai** ('Salt is also added to dhansak') and **kaar Thiik kar dii gaii hai** ('The car has been repaired').

So you can see that 'second helping' **jaa** can be in the **-taa** or **-aa** (or any other) form, and of course combine with any form of **hai, thaa, hogaa** etc.

HELPING chuk – 'COMPLETELY COMPLETE'

'First helping' **jaa** suggests the completion of an action, but if you really want to *stress* the point use **chuk** instead. When Rizwana says **tab se aaj tak mā̃i kaii kaam kar** *chukii hū̃* – 'Since then I've done many jobs' – the sense is that she has gained considerable breadth of experience. **chuk**, like **sak** (Unit 7), combines with a main verb in the *stem form*, and can never stand on its own as a main verb itself. It is also 'intransitive', so in the **-aa** form agrees with the subject.

'JOINING UP' WITH 'HELPING' kar

Probably the most commonly used 'helping verb' of all in Hindi and Urdu is **-kar**, which is added to the *stem form* of the main verb. You use it to link separate verbs together in one sentence. For example Mr Kazi wants to tell Omar that he went back to Pakistan (**mā̃i paakistaan vaapas gayaa**) and that he ran his own business there

(**maĩne apnaa kaarobaar kiyaa**). He links these two ideas together in one sentence by using **-kar** after the *stem form* of the main verb (**jaa**) of the first sentence: **paakistaan vaapas** *jaakar* **maĩne apnaa kaarobaar kiyaa** – 'After going back to Pakistan I ran my own business', or 'I went back to Pakistan and ran my own business'.

As the following example shows, you can use 'helping' **kar** more than once in the same sentence. In fact as long as you have breath in your body you can use it to *join up* as many verbs as you like in one sentence: **aap us kamre mẽ jaakar kursii par baiThkar chaay piijiye** ('Please go into that room, take a seat, and have a cup of tea'). 'Helping' **kar** is sometimes shortened to **ke** – particularly when the main verb is also **kar: maĩ kaam karke ghar jaaũ̃ugaa** ('I shall go home after I've done the work').

EXERCISES

1

Personal details

Budding actress Uma Patel is being interviewed by a reporter for a film magazine, looking for 'human interest' stories. Check Uma's cv against what she actually says. How often does she stick to the facts (☑), and how often does she 'stretch the truth' (☒)?

CURRICULUM VITAE

Name: Uma Patel
Date of birth: 10/5/65
Place of birth: Nairobi

EDUCATION:
1970–1976   Primary School, Nairobi
1976–1983   Comprehensive School, Ilford   3 'A', 7 'O' levels
1983–1986   University of Bath   BA Music & Theatre
1987–1988   School of Drama, London   Diploma in Acting

HOBBIES & INTERESTS:
Travel – I spent a year travelling round India after graduating from university.
Music – I play the piano and the sitar.
Languages – I speak Gujarati, Hindi, and Urdu, as well as English.

ACTING EXPERIENCE TO DATE:
I have appeared in a series of television commercials for the Bath & Bristol Building Society.

Reporter:	**aap kahãã paidaa huii thĩĩ?**
Uma Patel:	**mãĩ** Nairobi **mẽ paidaa huii.** ☐ *a*
Reporter:	**to aapkii paRhaaii vahãã huii?**
Uma Patel:	**jii hãã, aThaaraa saal kii umr tak.** ☐ *b*
Reporter:	Kenya **mẽ kaafii zabaanẽ bolii jaatii hãĩ. aapko kitnii zabaanẽ aatii hãĩ?**
Uma Patel:	**pãã̃ch. gujaraatii, hindii, urduu,** Swahili, **aur angrezii.** ☐ *c*
Reporter:	**skuul ke baad aapne kyaa kiyaa?**
Uma Patel:	**skuul ke baad, jab mãĩ aThaaraa saal kii thii, tab mãĩ is mulk mẽ aa gaii.** ☐ *d*
Reporter:	**aur yahãã aakar aapne kyaa kiyaa?**
Uma Patel:	**yahãã aakar mãĩne** music and theatre **mẽ degree lii.** ☐ *e*
Reporter:	**to aapko sangiit bhii pasand hai?**
Uma Patel:	**jii hãã, mujhe Gazal gaane kaa, aur sitaar bajaane kaa bhii bahut shauK hai.** ☐ *f*
Reporter:	University **ke baad aapne kyaa kiyaa?**
Uma Patel:	**sab se pahle mãĩ ghuumne-phirne ke liye inDiyaa gaii.** ☐ *g* **uske baad yahãã vaapas aakar mãĩne** acting **kii** training **kii.** ☐ *h* **phir** actress **ban gaii aur tab se aaj tak mãĩ** theatre **mẽ bhii,** television **par bhii kaii kaam kar chukii hũũ.** ☐ *i*

2

Go-between

Dominique Delon has just moved in next-door. You invite her round for a cup of tea. Your neighbour on the other side, Mohinder Sharma (with whom you normally speak in Hindi), comes in to say hello. They strike up a conversation through you:

a   Mohinder asks you **ye kahãã paidaa huii thĩĩ?** What do you ask Dominique (in English)?

b   Dominique replies that she was born in Paris. What do you say to Mohinder (in Hindi)?

c   Mohinder says **inkii paRhaaii kahãã huii?** What do you ask Dominique?

d   She says 'First of all in Paris, and after that in London.' What do you say to Mohinder?

e   Mohinder asks **jab ye** London **aaĩĩ, tab inkii umr kitnii thii?** What do you ask Dominique?

f   Dominique says she was ten years old at the time. What do you say to Mohinder?

g   He asks **skuul ke baad inhõne kyaa kiyaa?** What do you ask Dominique?

h   She says she went back to Paris and worked in a department store for a year. What do you say to Mohinder?

i   He asks **aur uske baad inhõne kyaa kiyaa?** What do you ask

Dominique?

j   She says she then came back to this country, and since then she's done a lot of different jobs here. What do you say to Mohinder?

3
'Help!'

In this story about Dharminder Singh and his sister, Kamaljit Kaur, the 'helping' verbs **le, de, sak, jaa,** and **chuk** are missing. Fill in the gaps with the right **-taa, -aa,** or other form of one of these verbs:

kamaljiit aur dharmindar panjaab mẽ paidaa hue, magar jab chhoTe the tab apne maataa pitaa ke saath yahãã is mulk mẽ aa _____ (jaa). skuul mẽ kamaljiit ne bahut mehnat kii. usne biology, maths, **aur** chemistry **mẽ tiin** 'A' levels (masc.) **le _____ (le). skuul ke baad** university **mẽ** medicine **paRhkar vo DaakTar ban _____ (jaa).**

    dharmindar bhii skuul kii paRhaaii kar _____ (chuk) hai. use zabaanẽ siikhne kaa shauK hai. uske paas English, French **aur panjaabii mẽ** 'A' levels **hãĩ, aur vo urduu aur hindii bhii bol _____ (sak) hai. skuul ke baad usne apnaa kaarobaar shuruu kar _____ (le). uske baad ek saal ke liye panjaab jaakar phir yahãã vaapas aa _____ (jaa). tab se aaj tak vo kaii kaam kar _____ (chuk) hai. ab usne bhii** university **mẽ** degree course **ke liye** application (fem.) **de _____ (de) hai.** university **mẽ tiin saal paRhkar vo bhii** degree **le _____ (le).**

4
Getting spliced

These pairs of sentences are all perfectly grammatical, but they're itching to be joined up together. Make one sentence out of two using the **kar** or **ke** form. The first one has been done for you.

a   **mãĩne chaay pii. uske baad mãĩ baahar gayaa.**
    mãĩ chaay piikar baahar gayaa.

b   **aap** London **gaĩĩ. uske baad aapne kyaa kiyaa?**

c   **vo is mulk mẽ vaapas aaẽge. phir vo apnaa kaarobaar shuruu karẽge.**

d   **mãĩ urduu siikh rahii hũũ. uske baad mãĩ paakistaan jaanaa chaahtii hũũ.**

e   **aapkaa bachchaa ye davaaii legaa. phir vo Thiik ho jaaegaa.**

f   **mãĩne mirch-masaalaa Khariidaa. uske baad mãĩne achchhaa khaanaa banaayaa.**

g   **ham khaanaa khaaẽge. uske baad ham** television **dekhẽge.**

h   **usne kaam kiyaa. phir vo vaapas gaii.**

i   **mãĩ baahar jaa rahaa hũũ. mãĩ fuTbaal khelnaa chaahtaa hũũ.**

mãĩne thoRii hindii siikhii hai. ab mãĩ hindustaanii dostõ ke saath baat-chiit kar saktii hũu.

5
A question of relativity

Some of the words <u>underlined</u> in the English sentences below are question-words and some are 'relative'. How would you translate these words into Hindi and Urdu – with a **k-** or **j-** word? (The full translations are given in the exercise key.)

a	<u>What</u> is your name?	**j/k**
b	<u>Where</u> do you live?	**j/k**
c	I live <u>where</u> you work.	**j/k**
d	How old were you <u>when</u> you came here?	**j/k**
e	<u>How</u> old were you when you went back?	**j/k**
f	<u>What kind</u> of food do you like?	**j/k**
g	I like food in <u>which</u> there are a lot of spices.	**j/k**
h	<u>Which</u> films do you like?	**j/k**
i	Do you like the music <u>which</u> they play in the films?	**j/k**

6
Passive agreement

These passive sentences are missing their 'helping' verbs. Select from among the choices in the right hand column to complete each sentence. For sentences a–d choose from among 1–4 and for e–h from 5–8.

a	**is mulk mẽ kaafii zabaanẽ bolii**	1	**jaataa hai**
b	**hindustaanii khaane mẽ bahut masaale Daale**	2	**jaatii hai**
c	**is** factory **mẽ kaii kaam kiye**	3	**jaate hãĩ**
d	Wembley Stadium **mẽ fuTbaal khelaa**	4	**jaatii hãĩ**
e	**dopahar kaa khaanaa khaa liyaa**	5	**gayaa hai**
f	**usko tiin chiTThiyãã likhii**	6	**gaii hai**
g	**pulaav banaayaa**	7	**gae hãĩ**
h	**mere bachchõ ko angrezii sikhaaii**	8	**gaii hãĩ**

7
The teacher's story

Clive Morgan's account of his life to date has got mixed up. Look out for **sab se pahle, phir, ke baad, jab . . . tab . . .** and the **-kar** form to help you put it in the right order.

a **vaapas aakar mãĩne** Manchester **mẽ angrezii paRhaane kaa kaam kiyaa. phir mãĩ** Community Language Teacher **bhii ban gayaa. angrezii ke saath-saath mãĩne hindii, urduu, aur bangaalii bhii paRhaaii.**

b   **skuul ke baad mãĩ** university **gayaa. jab mãĩ** university **mẽ thaa tab mãĩ ek saal ke liye** India **mẽ bhii rahaa, aur us vaKt mãĩne phir se urduu aur hindii siikhnii shuruu kĩ. phir vaapas aakar mãĩne 1979 mẽ** South Asian Studies **mẽ degree lii.**

c   **mãĩ** Cardiff **mẽ paidaa huaa, magar jab mãĩ chhoTaa thaa tab mãĩ apne vaalid, vaalidaa, aur bhaaiiõ ke saath** India **gayaa. chaar saal kii umr tak mãĩ vahãã rahaa. us vaKt mujhe hindii, gujaraatii, aur angrezii aatii thĩ.**

d   **uske baad mãĩ** Cardiff **vaapas aayaa. ab mãĩ angrezii paRhaa rahaa hũũ aur** Welsh **siikh rahaa hũũ.**

e   **sab se pahle mãĩ** Bangladesh **gayaa. vahãã mãĩne do saal angrezii paRhaaii, aur thoRii bangaalii bhii siikh lii. uske baad mãĩne** India **vaapas jaakar hindii mẽ diploma liyaa. phir mãĩ yahãã vaapas aayaa.**

f   **uske baad mãĩ yahãã vaapas aayaa, aur merii paRhaaii is mulk mẽ huii. skuul mẽ mãĩne angrezii,** French, **aur sangiit mẽ 'A' levels liye.**

g   University **ke baad mãĩne** teacher training **kii, aur tab se aaj tak mãĩ kaii kaam kar chukaa hũũ.**

 8

Listening exercise

Three people ask you for help in filling in application forms. Listen to their life stories and then fill in a form like this for them.

NAME:
ADDRESS:

EDUCATION:

WORK EXPERIENCE:

BACKGROUND

NEWSPAPERS, RADIO, TELEVISION AND OTHER RESOURCES

By now we hope you will have decided to learn to read and to write Hindi or Urdu, or preferably both. Once you have acquired a basic literacy, your language learning will accelerate rapidly as you will be able to use printed matter as well as the spoken word as learning material. You will also have taken the first step to gaining access to a wealth of poetry and literature.

Omar reading the *Daily Jang*.

One important potential resource is newspapers and periodicals. Urdu is particularly well served in Britain in this regard. There are daily newspapers (e.g. *Daily Jang*), plus weeklies and other periodicals. There is also a Hindi weekly (*Amardeep*). These papers carry news and advertising of particular interest to Asian readers in Britain as well as news from the subcontinent. You might like to try reading just the advertisements at first. The print is often larger and easier to read and you may find that large numbers of English words are used. If you're a film fan you'll be pleased to know you can also get British-based film magazines in Hindi and Urdu.

For the spoken word check with your local radio stations as many have programmes aimed at Asian listeners, some of which will be in Hindi and Urdu. Many of these programmes are music programmes, so even if the presenters use English you'll still get a chance to hear Hindi and Urdu songs. BBC World Service also broadcasts in Hindi and Urdu to India and Pakistan.

Remember also to keep an eye on the TV columns. Hindi and Urdu films, subtitled in English, are shown from time to time as are television soaps from India and Pakistan.

Finally, you should be at the stage now where, if you do want to take either or both of these languages further, a good grammar book and dictionaries would be useful to you. You won't find Romanised dictionaries anywhere, which is another good reason for learning to read both Hindi and Urdu. The following dictionaries are quite comprehensive:

Hindi–English: *hindii-angrezii kosh* by Brij Mohan and Badrinath Kapoor (Meenakshi Prakashan, New Delhi)
English–Hindi: *angrezii-hindii kosh* by Fr. C. Bulcke (S. Chand & Co, New Delhi)
Urdu–English: Standard Twentieth Century Dictionary by Bashir Ahmed Qureshi (Educational Publishing House, Lahore)
English–Urdu: Standard Twentieth Century Dictionary by Bashir Ahmed Qureshi (Educational Publishing House, Lahore)

There are plenty of grammar books of Hindi and Urdu available. R. S. McGregor's *Outline of Hindi Grammar* (Oxford University Press, New Delhi) offers a detailed description of the language with supporting translation exercises. One of the volumes of Ralph Russell's *Course in Urdu and Spoken Hindi* (SOAS, London) also deals with the grammar of the language. Both these authors use slightly different systems of Romanisation from the one used in this book.

Review 2

EXTENDED LISTENING PRACTICE

In the space of just ten units we've covered a lot of ground, particularly in the second half of this course. Don't worry if you feel you haven't mastered every detail. You shouldn't expect to learn a whole new language in just a few weeks! But if you now feel able at least to *understand* some of the Hindi and Urdu you hear around you, and perhaps try *using* them yourself in some common situations too, then you can consider yourself to have successfully passed the first hurdle in learning these languages.

This final listening passage is just to consolidate everything you've done so far. It brings together most, if not all, of the things you've learnt. It's long and wide-ranging, so the first two or three times you listen to it you might like to read the script at the same time (with the parallel translation!), or at least have it close to hand to check up on unfamiliar items. But there are no new words in it that haven't been introduced in either the units or *Review 1*. There are no tasks to do while listening either – no notes to take, no pictures to draw, no charts to fill. Just sit back and enjoy it – as many times as you like. Good luck!

'BEGINNER'S BOL CHAAL'

Lorraine Stevens is starting a new job today at Khetibari Urban Farm Produce Ltd. Khetibari controls a number of allotments around the city where people like supervisor Joginder Singh Parmar and gardener Wali Khan grow herbs and vegetables to supply to local retail outlets. Lorraine has just arrived at the office to meet her new boss, Khetibari manager Asha Chauhan. Asha decides to show her round 'The Farm'.

In the office:
(Door knock)

Asha: **aaiye.**

(Door knock)

Asha: **aaiye, andar aaiye.**

(Door opens)

Lorraine: Oh hello . . . er . . . **meraa naam** Lorraine Stevens **hai.**

Asha: What? Oh, Lorraine Stevens . . . **kyaa aapko hindii aatii hai?**

Lorraine: **bahut kam. skuul mẽ mãĩne thoRii urduu siikhii thii. mãĩ hindii bhii bol saktii hũũ, magar paRh nahĩĩ saktii.**

Asha: **bahut achchhaa, bahut achchhaa! aapse milkar mujhe baRii Khushii huii.**

Lorraine: **bahut meharbaanii.**

Asha: **aap hindii aur urduu kab se siikh rahii hãĩ?**

Loraine: **tiin saal se.**

Asha: **tiin saal se hii! magar aapkii hindii bahut achchhii hai!**

Lorraine: **achchhaa?**

Asha: **hãã, bahut achchhii hai, bahut achchhii hai . . . achchhaa, aaj hamaare** supervisor, Mr Parmar, office **nahĩĩ aae. vo kahãã hai? . . .** Lorraine, **kyaa aap hamaaraa** 'farm' **dekhnaa chaahtii hãĩ?**

Lorraine: **jii hãã**

Asha: **mere saath aaiye . . .**

At the allotment:

Wali Khan: Parmar **saahab, kaise hãĩ?**

Joginder Parmar: oh Khan **saahab! aaj mãĩ Thiik nahĩĩ hũũ. tabiiyat kaafii Kharaab hai.**

Khan: **kyaa baat hai?**

Parmar: **maaluum nahĩĩ. thoRaa sar-dard hai, magar buKhaar nahĩĩ hai. meraa galaa bhii Kharaab hai, magar mujhe khããsii nahĩĩ.**

Khan: **achchhaa? aapko sardii nahĩĩ lagii?**

Parmar: **sardii kaise? kal to mãĩ ghar mẽ hii thaa. mãĩ baahar nahĩĩ gayaa.**

Khan: **hãã, magar ye sardii kaa mausam gharõ ke andar bhii aataa hai. mere Khayaal mẽ aapko sardii lagii hai.**

Parmar: **achchhaa?**

Khan: **hãã, is mulk kaa mausam mere liye bhii Thiik nahĩĩ hai.**

Parmar: **aapke liye Thiik nahĩĩ hai, mere liye bhii Thiik nahĩĩ hai. magar ham kyaa karẽ? kaam to karnaa hii hai, bhaaii saahab.**

Khan: **jii hãã, kaam to karnaa hai, magar ek aur saal ke baad mãĩ paakistaan vaapas jaaũũgaa!**

Parmar: **achchhaa, aapko vaapas jaanaa hai?**

Khan: **jii hãã, mujhe** Peshawar **vaapas jaanaa hai.**

Parmar: Peshawar? **aap** Peshawar **se hãĩ?**

Khan: **hãã,** Peshawar **se hii. . . .**

	In the office:
	(Door knock)
Asha:	Come.
	(Door knock)
Asha:	Come, come in.
	(Door opens)
Lorraine:	Oh, hello . . . er . . . my name is Lorraine Stevens.
Asha:	What? Oh, Lorraine Stevens . . . Do you speak Hindi?
Lorraine:	Very little. At school I learnt a little Urdu. I can speak a little Hindi too, but I can't read it.
Asha:	Very good! Very good! I'm very pleased to meet you.
Lorraine:	Thank you.
Asha:	How long have you been learning Urdu?
Lorraine:	For three years.
Asha:	Just three years! But your Hindi is very good!
Lorraine:	Really?
Asha:	Yes, it's very good, very good . . . Right, our supervisor, Mr Parmar hasn't come to the office today. Where is he? . . . Lorraine, would you like to see our 'farm'?
Lorraine:	Yes please.
Asha:	Come with me . . .

	At the allotment:
Wali Khan:	Mr Parmar, how are you?
Joginder Parmar:	Oh Mr Khan! I'm not well today. I'm quite sick.
Khan:	What's the problem?
Parmar:	I don't know. I have a slight headache, but no temperature. I have a sore throat as well, but no cough.
Khan:	Really? You haven't caught a cold?
Parmar:	How? Yesterday I was in all day. I didn't go out.
Khan:	Yes, but this cold weather gets indoors too. I think you've caught a cold.
Parmar:	Really?
Khan:	Yes, the weather in this country is no good for me either.
Parmar:	It's no good for you, and it's no good for me either. But what can we do? We have to work, brother.
Khan:	Yes, we have to work, but after one more year I'll go back to Pakistan.
Parmar:	Really? You're going back?
Khan:	Yes, I'm going back to Peshawar.
Parmar:	Peshawar? You're from Peshawar?
Khan:	Yes, from Peshawar itself. . .

In Asha's car:

Asha: **aapne urduu skuul mẽ siikhii,** Lorraine. **bahut achchhii baat hai. aapkii paRhaaii yahãã is mulk mẽ huii?**

Lorraine: **jii hãã. mere maataa-pitaa** Trinidad **se aae, magar mãĩ yahãã is mulk mẽ paidaa huii.**

Asha: **aapke pitaajii kyaa kaam karte hãĩ?**

Lorraine: **vo** college **mẽ** lab technician **hãĩ.**

Asha: **unko bhii hindii aatii hai?**

Lorraine: **jii nahĩĩ, magar maataajii kɔ thoRii bhojpurii hindii aatii hai.**

Asha: **vo kaise?**

Lorraine: **unke daadaajii hindustaan se** Trinidad **aae the.**

Asha: **achchhaa, aap kitne bhaaii-bahanẽ hãĩ?**

Lorraine: **ham do hii hãĩ – mãĩ aur mere baRe bhaaii.**

Asha: **aapke bhaaii kahãã rahte hãĩ?**

Lorraine: **vo hamaare saath rahte hãĩ. vo** police officer **hãĩ.**

Asha: **achchhaa, bhaaii saahab** policeman **hãĩ. bahut achchhaa . . . aur aapke kyaa kyaa shauK hãĩ,** Lorraine?

Lorraine: **shauK?**

Asha: **hãã, kyaa aapko tairnaa pasand hai, yaa filmẽ dekhnaa pasand hai, yaa giTaar bajaanaa pasand hai? . . . aapke kyaa kyaa shauK hãĩ?**

Lorraine: **achchhaa, shauK. mujhe filmẽ dekhne kaa shauK hai aur sangiit sunne kaa bhii shauK hai.**

Asha: **aapko kis Kism kaa sangiit pasand hai?**

Lorraine: **mujhe Khaas taur par bhangRaa pasand hai. bhangRaa mujhe bahut achchhaa lagtaa hai.**

Asha: **achchhaa, bhangRaa . . . magar aap** daytime discos **to nahĩĩ jaatĩĩ?**

Lorraine: **jii?** Er . . . **jii nahĩĩ, nahĩĩ jaatii.**
   (car stops)

Asha: **achchhaa, dekhiye, ham aaii hãĩ. hamaare** supervisor Mr Parmar **kahãã hãĩ? . . . aah vahãã hãĩ,** Wali Khan **ke saath. oho, . . . vo donõ bolte bahut hãĩ, magar kaam bahut kam karte hãĩ . . .**

At the allotment

Khan: **ye kaun aa rahii hãĩ?**

Parmar: **ek to hamaarii** manager **hãĩ. magar unke saath kaun hãĩ?**

Asha: Hello Mr Parmar, Mr Khan, **kyaa haal hai?**

Khan: **buraa to nahĩĩ hai, jii . . .**

Asha: **magar achchhaa bhii nahĩĩ. mujhe maaluum hai,** Khan **saahab. achchhaa, suniye. ye hamaarii** secretary **hãĩ,** Ms Lorraine Stevens, **aur inko urduu bhii, aur hindii bhii aatii hãĩ.** Lorraine **ye** Mr Wali Khan **hãĩ.**

In Asha's car:

Asha: You learnt Urdu in school, Lorraine. Very good. Did you go to school here in this country?

Lorraine: Yes. My parents come from Trinidad, but I was born here in this country.

Asha: What does your father do?

Lorraine: He's a lab technician in the college.

Asha: Does he also speak Hindi?

Lorraine: No. But my mother knows a little Bhojpuri Hindi.

Asha: How come?

Lorraine: Her grandfather came to Trinidad from India.

Asha: I see. How many brothers and sisters have you got?

Lorraine: There are just two of us – myself and my brother.

Asha: Where does your brother live?

Lorraine: He lives with us. He's a police officer.

Asha: I see. Your brother's a policeman. Very good . . . and what are your hobbies Lorraine?

Lorraine: Hobbies?

Asha: Yes, do you like swimming, or watching films, or playing the guitar? . . . What are your hobbies?

Lorraine: Oh, hobbies. I like watching films and listening to music too.

Asha: What kind of music do you like?

Lorraine: I particularly like bhangra. I think it's great.

Asha: Oh really, bhangra . . . But you don't go to daytime discos?

Lorraine: Sorry? Er . . . no, no I don't.
(car stops)

Asha: Right, look we've arrived. Where's our supervisor Mr Parmar? . . . Oh there he is, with Wali Khan. Oh dear, those two talk a lot but do very little . . .

At the allotment:

Khan: Who are these coming?

Parmar: One is our manager. But who's with her?

Asha: Hello Mr Parmar, Mr Khan. How are things?

Khan: Not too bad . . .

Asha: But not too good either. I know, Mr Khan. Right, listen. This is our secretary, Ms Lorraine Stevens, and she speaks Hindi and Urdu. Lorraine, this is Mr Wali Khan.

Lorraine:	assalaam alaikum.
Khan:	vaalaikum assalaam.
Asha:	aur ye Mr Parmar hãĩ.
Lorraine:	sat srii akaal.
Parmar:	sat srii akaal.
Asha:	achchhaa Mr Parmar, Lorraine Khetibari **kaa kaam dekhnaa chaahtii hãĩ.**
Parmar:	aaiye, . . . dekhiye . . .

Lorraine:	ye kyaa hai?
Parmar:	ye muulii hai.
Lorraine:	aur ye kyaa hai?
Parmar:	ye dhaniyaa hai.
Lorraine:	dhaniyaa? isko angrezii mẽ kyaa kahte hãĩ?
Parmar:	maaluum nahĩĩ. mujhe angrezii nahĩĩ aatii.
Lorraine:	angrezii nahĩĩ aatii? aap kahãã paidaa hue the?
Parmar:	Punjab mẽ, aur merii paRhaaii bhii vahãã huii.
Lorraine:	skuul ke baad aapne kyaa kiyaa?
Parmar:	skuul ke baad mãĩne apnaa kaarobaar shuruu kiyaa. phir mãĩ yahãã is mulk mẽ aa gayaa, aur yahãã aakar mãĩ kaii kaam kar chukaa hũũ . . .

Lorraine:	. . . achchhaa Mr Parmar **bahut shukriyaa. ab mujhe** office **vaapas jaanaa hai. sat srii akaal.**
Parmar:	sat srii akaal.
Asha:	achchhaa, Lorraine, **aapko hamaaraa** Khetibari Urban Farm **kaisaa lagtaa hai?**
Lorraine:	bahut achchhaa lagtaa hai. bahut bahut achchhaa.

Lorraine:	Hello.
Khan:	Hello.
Asha:	And this is Mr Parmar.
Lorraine:	Hello.
Parmar:	Hello.
Asha:	Right Mr Parmar. Lorraine wants to see the work that Khetibari does.
Parmar:	Come with me . . . Have a look . . .

Lorraine:	What's this?
Parmar:	This is radish.
Lorraine:	And what's this?
Parmar:	This is 'dhaniya'.
Lorraine:	'dhaniya'? What's it called in English?
Parmar:	I don't know. I can't speak English.
Lorraine:	You don't know English? Where were you born?
Parmar:	In the Punjab. And I was educated there too.
Lorraine:	What did you do when you left school?
Parmar:	After school I started my own business. Then I came to this country. And since coming here I've done many different jobs . . .

Lorraine:	. . . Well thank you very much Mr Parmar. I have to go back to the office now. Goodbye.
Parmar:	Goodbye.
Asha:	So, Lorraine, what do you think of our Khetibari Urban Farm?
Lorraine:	I like it, very very much.

Grammatical summary

You can learn to speak a language well (as children do) without a *conscious* knowledge of the rules of its grammar. In fact, good and fluent speakers of a language never *consciously* construct their sentences according to rules of grammar. But it is always convenient for adult learners (who already know at least one other language) to know some of the important rules which they can *consciously* make use of in order to *speed up* their learning. This section is meant to provide you with handy tools to help you do this. It covers only those aspects of Hindi and Urdu grammar which relate to the structures you have learnt. (And, of course, there are some complicated Hindi and Urdu structures which could not be taught at this stage.) The grammatical framework presented here is fairly traditional, though you will find that in many ways Hindi and Urdu grammar is quite different from the English grammar you may be familiar with.

Use this section in conjunction with and to supplement the more detailed explanations given in the *How the Language Works* sections of the main units.

NOUNS

As in the other Indo-European languages (English, French, German etc), a noun in Hindi and Urdu *names* persons, objects, places, abstract notions etc.

GENDER

Every noun in Hindi and Urdu (as in French and Spanish) is either masculine or feminine. Male animate beings are nearly always masculine and female animate beings are nearly always feminine. But there is no general rule to determine the gender of inanimate objects, places and abstract notions. There is no reason on earth why **pyaaz** (onion), **kamraa** (room), **peT** (stomach), **dard** (pain) and **laahaur** (Lahore) should be masculine, and **paalak** (spinach), **khiRkii** (window), **ãakh** (eye), **khãasii** (cough), and

dillii (Delhi) should be feminine. The only advice we can give is that when you learn a new noun word, you should also learn whether it is masculine or feminine.

Most nouns ending in **-aa** are masculine and most nouns ending in **-ii** are feminine. **savaarii** (passenger), whether male or female, is always feminine, presumably because of the **-ii** ending. But there are glaring exceptions: **maalii** (gardener) is masculine and **maalaa** (garland) is feminine!

NUMBER

As in English, when a Hindi and Urdu noun refers to one person, object etc it is singular; when it refers to more than one person, object etc it is plural. **kamraa** (room) is singular and **kamre** (rooms) is plural. But the Hindi and Urdu ways of determining whether something is one or more than one may not be the same as in English. Objects like **Kãichii** (scissors) and **paayjaamaa/paajaamaa** are singular in Hindi and Urdu and plural in English. On the other hand, food grains like **chaaval** (rice) are plural in Hindi and Urdu but singular in English. However, the majority of the Hindi and Urdu nouns are like their English equivalents in this respect.

ARTICLES

Hindi and Urdu have no articles (the equivalents of the English *a*, *an* and *the*).

PRONOUNS

Words used in place of nouns to refer to persons, objects etc are called pronouns. The Hindi and Urdu pronouns are given in the *How the Language Works* section in Unit 1 in combination with **hũũ, hai, hãĩ** etc.

DEMONSTRATIVES

The third person pronouns of Hindi and Urdu are really demonstratives (the equivalents of the English *this*, *that*, *these* and *those*). Hence, there is a distinction of nearness and distance. Again like the English demonstratives, Hindi and Urdu **ye** and **vo** can be used as both pronouns and adjectives. (See below for what adjectives are.)

Pronoun **ye**   *ye* **kyaa hai?**
                              What is *this*?

Adjective **ye**   *ye* **kamraa baRaa hai.**
                              This room is big.

ADJECTIVES

Words which *describe* the qualities of objects, persons etc are called adjectives. In grammar, adjectives are said to *qualify* nouns or pronouns. Unlike English adjectives, but like French and Spanish adjectives, many Hindi and Urdu adjectives are marked for number and gender according to the number and gender of the noun they qualify.

BLACK AND RED ADJECTIVES

Adjectives in many North Indian languages including Hindi and Urdu can be divided into two classes – the Black and the Red adjectives. Black adjectives change their form to show number and gender (see *How the Language Works* in Unit 3) and also have oblique forms; Red adjectives do not change their form at all. The terms Red adjective and Black adjective are used because the Hindi and Urdu word **kaalaa** (black) is a typical Black adjective and **laal** (red) is a typical Red adjective!

It is very easy to determine the 'colour' of a Hindi and Urdu adjective. Adjectives which end in **-aa** (**kaalaa** 'black', **meraa** 'my', **baRaa** 'big, older', etc) are Black, and those which do not end in **-aa** (**laal** 'red', **mazbuut** 'strong', **gappii** 'talkative' etc) are Red.

It should be noted that in Black adjectives, the masculine singular and the masuline plural forms differ, but the feminine singular and the feminine plural forms are the same. Some nouns also change their form in a similar, but not identical, way.

POSSESSIVE ADJECTIVES

Hindi and Urdu possessive adjectives (the equivalents of the English *my, our, his, her* etc) are gramatically Black adjectives. They are

meraa my (from **mã͠i** 'I')
hamaaraa our (from **ham** 'we')
teraa your (from **tuu** 'you', *very* familiar)
tumhaaraa your (from **tum** 'you', familiar)
aapkaa your (from **aap** 'you', polite)
iskaa his/her/its (from **ye** 'he/she/it')
uskaa his/her/its (from **vo** 'he/she/it')
inkaa their (from **ye** 'they')
unkaa their (from **vo** 'they')
apnaa my, our, your, his, her, their (see Unit 7)

POSTPOSITIONS

I   SIMPLE POSTPOSITIONS

The Hindi and Urdu equivalents of the English prepositions (*in, on, at* etc) *follow*, and do not come before, a noun or pronoun. Hence Hindi and Urdu have *post*positions. The most commonly used postpositions in Hindi and Urdu are

mẽ   in
par   on
ko   to
se   from
tak   up to
kaa   of
nẽ   Special agent marker

Grammatically, **kaa** changes its form like a Black adjective.

II COMPOUND POSTPOSITIONS

Most compound postpositions consist of

ke + location expression (+ a simple postposition)

(The final simple postposition, which can occur in only a few combinations, is generally optional.) The most commonly used compound postpositions in Hindi and Urdu are

ke saamne	in front of
ke niiche	under
ke piichhe	behind
ke biich (mẽ)	between, in the middle of
ke darmyaan	between, in the middle of
ke andar	inside
ke baahar	outside
ke paas	near

There are other compound postpositions which are structured similarly but which do not have location meanings. Some of these postpositions are

ke liye	for/for the sake of
kii Khaatir	for/for the sake of
ke baad	after (in time)
ke saath	with
se pahle	before

DIRECT AND OBLIQUE FORMS

A noun, pronoun or adjective followed by a postposition in Hindi and Urdu changes its form. The new form thus acquired is called the *oblique* form. The non-oblique or the original form is called the *direct* form. Examples are

meraa beTaa
direct direct
my son

mere beTe ko
oblique oblique postposition
to my son

mere beTe kaa kamraa
oblique oblique postposition direct direct
my son's room

mere beTe ke kamre mẽ
oblique oblique postposition oblique oblique postposition
in my son's room

kaa is the only postposition in Hindi and Urdu which can have an oblique form when followed by another postposition (**mẽ** in the above example).

As we shall see below, in the case of some nouns and adjectives, the direct and the oblique forms are identical.

DIRECT AND OBLIQUE FORMS OF NOUNS AND ADJECTIVES

How the Language Works in Unit 3 shows the four different noun classes of Hindi and Urdu and how they are marked for gender and number *in direct form only*.

But nouns (and *adjectives*) may also change form depending on whether or not they are followed by a postposition. If they are followed by a postposition, they take an *oblique* form. If not, they take the *direct* form. Here are some examples using the postposition **se** (from) with the Black adjective **meraa** (my) and the nouns **bhaaii**, **bahan**, **beTaa** and **beTii** from the four different classes. Red adjectives do not change.

Noun class			Direct	Oblique
Masculine	**-aa**	sg.	**meraa beTaa** my son	**mere beTe se** from my son
		pl.	**mere beTe** my sons	**mere beTõ se** from my sons
	non-**aa**	sg.	**meraa bhaaii** my brother	**mere bhaaii se** from my brother
		pl.	**mere bhaaii** my brothers	**mere bhaaiiõ se** from my brothers
Feminine	**-ii**	sg.	**merii beTii** my daughter	**merii beTii se** from my daughter
		pl.	**merii beTiyãã** my daughters	**merii beTiyõ se** from my daughters
	non-**ii**	sg.	**merii bahan** my sister	**merii bahan se** from my sister
		pl.	**merii bahanẽ** my sisters	**merii bahanõ se** from my sisters

Words like **pitaa**, **abbaa** (father), **chaachaa** (father's younger brother), **taayaa** (father's older brother), **maamaa** (mother's brother), **mausaa** (mother's sister's husband) and **phuuphaa** (father's sister's husband) – all male relatives – and **raajaa** (king, prince) are exceptions. These words are like those masculine nouns which don't end in **-aa**, for example **bhaaii**.

DIRECT AND OBLIQUE FORMS OF PRONOUNS

Gender distinctions are not marked on pronouns in Hindi and Urdu. But pronouns do have number distinction and direct and oblique forms. With all postpositions except **ne** (special agent marker), **ko** (to) and **kaa** (of), pronouns assume forms which can be called *general oblique* forms.

1   General oblique forms

	Direct form	Oblique form
First person	**mãĩ** I	**mujh (se)** (from) me
	ham we	**ham (se)** (from) us
Second person	**tuu** you	**tujh (se)** (from) you
	tum you	**tum (se)** (from) you
	aap you	**aap (se)** (from) you
Third person	**ye/yah** he/she/it	**is (se)** (from) him/her/it
	vo/vah he/she/it	**us (se)** (from) him/her/it
	ye they	**in (se)** (from) them
	vo/ve they	**un (se)** (from) them

2   Oblique forms with the postposition **ne**
With **ne** some pronouns have oblique forms which differ from the 'general oblique' forms. These forms are

	Direct form	Oblique form	
First person	**mãĩ** **ham**	**mãĩ (ne)** **ham (ne)**	(no change) (no change)
Second person	**tuu** **tum** **aap**	**tuu (ne)** **tum (ne)** **aap (ne)**	(no change) (no change) (no change)
Third person	**ye/yah** **vo/vah** **ye** **vo/ve**	**is (ne)** **us (ne)** **inhõ (ne)** **unhõ (ne)**	(general oblique) (general oblique) (special oblique) (special oblique)

3   Oblique forms with the postposition **ko** and dative forms
Many speakers of Hindi and Urdu have now started using the 'general' oblique forms of pronouns with the postposition **ko** (to) as well. But some speakers prefer older ('dative') forms of pronouns which already have the meaning of **ko** incorporated in them. So **ko** is not used with the 'dative' forms. You have the choice between:

mujhe/mujhko	to me
hamẽ/hamko	to us
tujhe/tujhko	to you
tumhẽ/tumko	to you
ise/isko	to him/her/it
use/usko	to him/her/it
inhẽ/inko	to them
unhẽ/unko	to them

But there is no 'dative' form of **aapko** in modern Hindi and Urdu.

QUESTION WORDS

All Hindi and Urdu question words begin with **k**:

kyaa	what
kaun	who
kab	when
kahãã	where
kyõ	why
kaisaa	how (Like what?)
kaise	how

kyaa and **kaun** are pronouns and **kaisaa** is an adjective. So these words change their form like other pronouns or adjectives. The other question words don't change their form.

VERBS

The last thing you should look for in the grammar of any North Indian language is a list of 'tenses' as you may find in traditional grammars of European languages. There is only one verb in Hindi and Urdu (**hai**) whose forms (**hai**, **thaa** etc) consistently refer to the present or the past time. So only this verb has the present and the past tenses. **hai** does not have any of the **-taa** or **-aa** or **-naa** forms or the subjunctive form.

THE VERB hai
1   Present tense forms
How the Language Works in Unit 1 lists the present tense forms of this verb. They are marked only for *person* and *number*.

2   Past tense forms
The past tense forms of this verb are marked only for *number and gender*. They are listed in *How the Language Works* in Unit 6.

VERBS OTHER THAN hai
The other verbs of Hindi and Urdu do not have present and past tense forms. They do not locate an action or event in time. That function is left to

hai and **thaa**. The forms given below are used to convey *different* kinds of meanings:

1 Order or request forms
There are different ways of giving orders and making requests. *How the Language Works* in Unit 5 shows the most polite way. But you may come across some other forms as well:

(tuu) jaa   (You) go! (Order)
Stem form only

(tum) jaao   (You) go! (Order/advice)
Stem + **o**

(aap) jaaiye   (You please) go (Polite request)
Stem + **iye**

There are some irregular **-iye** forms:

liijiye   (from **le** take)
diijiye   (from **de** give)
kiijiye   (from **kar** do)
piijiye   (from **pii** drink)

2   -taa form
The **-taa** form refers to an *uncompleted* action or event. A habitual or ongoing action is regarded as uncompleted. It is an adjectival form as, like an adjective, it is marked for number and gender (see *How the Language Works* in Unit 2).

3   -aa form
This form is also adjectival (see *How the Language Works* in Unit 6). But it refers to a *completed* action. Most often it refers to past (and, therefore, completed actions). But it can also refer to future actions which are so definite that they are thought of as already completed. So it is not really the same as a past tense form.

There are some irregular forms. The most important of these are

Stem	Masculine Singular	Masculine Plural	Feminine Singular	Feminine Plural
jaa	**gayaa**	**gae**	**gaii**	**gaı̃ı̃**
kar	**kiyaa**	**kiye**	**kii**	**kı̃ı̃**
le	**liyaa**	**liye**	**lii**	**lı̃ı̃**
de	**diyaa**	**diye**	**dii**	**dı̃ı̃**
ho	**huaa**	**hue**	**huii**	**huı̃ı̃**

4   -naa form
There are two kinds of **-naa** form. One of them is a straightforward masculine noun (see *How the Language Works* in Unit 8). The other (see Unit 9) refers to plans, obligations, impending events etc usually in the future. But it can refer to present or past plans etc as well.

5   Subjunctive form

This verb form refers to a potential, rather than actual, action or event. It is personal because, like the present tense form of **hai**, it is marked for *person* and number. But it is *not* a present tense form. So the verb endings are different from those added to **hai**. They are listed in *How the Language Works* in Unit 9.

There are some irregular verbs like **de** (give) and **le** (take) and **ho** (become/happen)

	de	le	ho
mãĩ	dũũ	lũũ	hũũ
tuu	de	le	ho
ye/vo	de	le	ho
ham	dẽ	lẽ	hõ
tum	do	lo	ho
ye/vo/aap	dẽ	lẽ	hõ

6   **gaa** form

One (remember, just one) of the ways of referring to a future action is to add the auxiliary **gaa** (which is marked for *number* and *gender*) to the subjunctive form. The combined form is thus marked for *person*, *gender* and *number* (twice). (See *How the Language Works* in Unit 9.)

HELPING VERBS

Hindi and Urdu 'helping verbs' are verbs which play a 'helping' role to the *main* verb of the sentence. They add to or modify its meaning in different ways and may combine with the main verb in various forms. There is a large number of such verbs in Hindi and Urdu. These are some of the commonest:

Form of main verb	Helping verb	Additional meaning
Stem	**de**	do for someone else
Stem	**le**	do for oneself
Stem	**rahaa**	ongoingness
Stem	**jaa**	completion
-aa	**jaa**	'passive voice'
Stem	**sak**	capability
Stem	**chuk**	emphasise completion
Stem	**kar**	completion of one action or event before another

SOME COMMON VERB COMBINATIONS: A ROUGH GUIDE

In Hindi and Urdu, literally hundreds of different combinations of main verbs and helping verbs with or without **hai** or **thaa** are possible. But you don't need to memorise every possible combination! If you know the most basic meaning of each verb form and the helping verbs, the overall meaning of the whole phrase should be quite clear. Here is a list of common and simple combinations using the main verb **aa** (come) with a first person singular masculine subject, together with rough English equivalents:

1 **-taa + hai**
   mãĩ aataa hũũ   I come

2 **-taa + thaa**
   mãĩ aataa thaa   I used to come

3 **-taa**
   mãĩ aataa   I'd have come

(Since the most basic meaning of the **-taa** form is 'uncompleted', the **-taa** form without any **hai** or **thaa** refers to an action that was not completed.)

4 **-aa + hai**
   mãĩ aayaa hũũ   I have come

5 **-aa + thaa**
   mãĩ aayaa thaa   I had come

6 **-aa**
   mãĩ aayaa   I came

7 Stem + **rahaa + hai**
   mãĩ aa rahaa hũũ   I'm coming

8 Stem + **rahaa + thaa**
   mãĩ aa rahaa thaa   I was coming

9 Subjunctive
   mãĩ aaũũ   I may come

10 Subjunctive + **gaa**
    mãĩ aaũũgaa   I'll come

11 Stem + **rahaa** + (Subjunctive form of **ho + gaa**)
    mãĩ aa rahaa hũũgaa   I'll be coming

A Guide to Hindi and Urdu pronunciation

We are not using the Hindi or Urdu script in this book. The Romanised transcript we are using represents Hindi and Urdu pronunciation *consistently* in the sense that a particular letter or combination of letters (except when the word has the **h** sound, for which see the *Sound Systems* section in Unit 2) always represents the same sound. The following letters and combinations of letters are used for transcribing Hindi and Urdu words in this book. Sometimes their pronunciation in Hindi and Urdu is not the same as in English. The English equivalents given are those of standard southern English except where otherwise indicated.

Letter(s)	Rough English equivalent sound	Hindi and Urdu example
VOWELS		
a	'a' as in 'about'	**ab**
aa	'a' as in 'calm'	**aap**
i	'i' as in 'bit'	**is**
ii	'ea' as in 'bead'	**hii**
u	'u' as in 'put'	**umr**
uu	'oo' as in 'food'	**uupar**
e	Scottish pronunciation of 'ai' as in 'laid'.	**meraa**
ai	Like but longer than 'a' as in 'bad'.	**jaisaa**
o	Scottish pronunciation of 'o' as in 'road'.	**ko**
au	Like but longer than 'o' as in 'cod'.	**kaun**
~ or ˜ . . .	This symbol can be added to any of the vowel symbols given above. It represents nasalisation. The vowel sound is produced both through the mouth and the nose, as French vowels sometimes are.	**hãã** **gaĩĩ** **mẽ** **mãĩ**

CONSONANTS

k	'k' as in 'skin'	**kaam**
kh	'k' as in 'kin' but with a short but strong burst of air. **k** and **kh** are different sounds and must be kept distinct in pronunciation. This applies to all the pairs distinguished by the presence of strong breath symbolised by **h**.	**khaanaa**
g........	'g' as in 'gun'	**gaanaa**
gh	Unlike any English consonant. Try pronouncing 'big house' as 'bi *gh*ouse'. A consonant sound pronounced with breathy voice.	**ghar**

ch......	'ch' as in 'eschew'	**chaar**
chh	'ch' as in 'cheese'. Same difference as in **k** and **kh**.	**chhe**
j........	'j' as in 'jug'	**jis**
jh.......	Try 'large house' as 'lar *jh*ouse'. Consonant sound with breathy voice.	**jhaag**

T	A bit like 't' in 'stop', but produced (like **Th**, **D** and **Dh**) by touching the top of the mouth with the underside of the curled tongue. (See diagram given at the end of this section.)	**TamaaTar**
Th	A bit like 't' in 'top'. Differs from **T** as **kh** differs from **k**.	**Thelaa**
D	A bit like 'd' in 'dog'	**Daal**
Dh	Try 'mad house' as 'ma *dh*ouse'. A consonant with breathy voice.	**Dhol**

t........	It is important not to confuse this group with the preceding one. These sounds are produced by touching the tip of the tongue against the front teeth. (See the diagram at the end of this section.) If you make the mistake of touching the ridge behind the teeth (as with English 't' and 'd') the distinction with the previous group will not be maintained.	**tum**
th.......	Differs from **t** as **kh** differs from **k** in the force of breath used.	**thaa**
d	Voiced sound. Differs from **t** as **g** differs from **k**.	**das**
dh	Consonant sound with breathy voice as in **gh**, **jh** and **Dh**.	**dho**
n	'n' as in 'nut'	**namak**

p	'p' as in 'spin'	**paas**
ph	'p' as in 'pin', but pronounced with strong breath force, as in **kh**, **th** etc.	**phal**
b	'b' as in 'bin'	**ban**
bh	Consonant with breathy voice. Try saying 'job hunt' as 'jo *bh*unt'.	**bhaashaa**
m	'm' as in 'man'	**muulii**
y	'y' as in 'yacht'	**yaa**
r	'r' as in 'red'	**rah**
l	'l' as in 'light'	**laal**
v	A bit like 'v' in 'vet', though the top teeth need not touch the bottom lip. So it may sound like 'w' as in 'wet'.	**vaalid**
sh	'sh' as in 'sheep'	**shaam**
s	's' as in 'sit'	**saath**
h	'h' as in 'hat'	**hai**
R	Like **D**, but flap your tongue forward so that the contact of the tongue with the roof of the mouth is only momentary.	**baRaa**
Rh	Like **Dh**, but flap your tongue forward as in **R**. Breathy voiced sound. Differs from **R** as **Dh** differs from **D**.	**paRhaa**
K	A bit like **k**, which is often used in its place, though **K** should be pronounced further back in the throat.	**Kism**
Kh	Like 'ch' in Scottish 'loch'. Sometimes replaced by **kh**.	**Khaas**
G	A voiced version of **Kh** which differs from **Kh** as **g** differs from **k**. Sometimes replaced by **g**.	**Gazal**
z	'z' as in 'zip'	**zukaam**
f	'f' as in 'fan'	**faaslaa**

Position of the tongue for Hindi and Urdu **T**, **Th**, **D**, **Dh**.

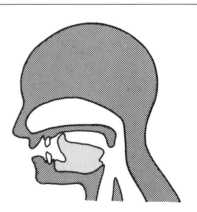

*Position of the tongue for Hindi and Urdu **t**, **th**, **d**, **dh**.*

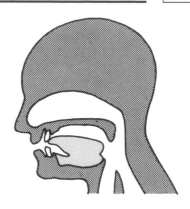

*Position of the tongue for English **t**, **d**. Avoid this tongue position in Hindi and Urdu if you want to keep (**T**, **Th**, **D**, **Dh**) and (**t**, **th**, **d**, **dh**) distinct in your speech.*

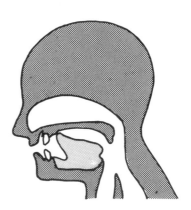

Key to exercises

UNIT 1

Check-ups:
1 Darshan Singh is a Sikh
2 A general enquiry
3 Harbans

1 Starting up
a namaste
b assalaam alaikum
c Hello (jii)
d aapkaa naam kyaa hai?
e kyaa haal hai?/aap kaise hãĩ?
f sat srii akaal

2 Answering back
a vaalaikum assalaam
b Thiik hai
c namaste
d meraa naam _____ hai.
e mãĩ Thiik hũũ.
f Hello jii
g sat srii akaal

3 How did it start
a kyaa haal hai?
b aapkaa naam kyaa hai?
c assalaam alaikum
d Thiik hai, aap kaisii hãĩ?

4 Is, am and are
a hai   b hai   c hũũ   d hãĩ

5 **Word search**
kaise, aapkaa, mãĩ, hãĩ, hai, jii, namaste, aap, kyaa, meraa, Thiik, bhii

6 **Crossword**
1 **mãĩ Thiik hũũ**
2 **bhii**
3 **kaisii**
4 **hai**
5 **kyaa**
6 **aap kaise hãĩ?**
7 **naam**
8 **assalaam alaikum**
Vertical Phrase: **Thiik hai**

7 **Listening exercise**
Muslim greetings. Imran Khan, Muhammad Ali. Both fine.

8 **Fill in the gaps**
a **hai** *b* **aapkaa** *c* **meraa** *d* **kyaa** *e* **hai**
f **hãĩ** *g* **bhii**

UNIT 2

Check-ups:
1 Minesh Shah
2 Sutton
3 By bus

1 **Who's who?**
Lawyer: Uma Joshi
Doctor: Kulwinder Kaur
Teacher: Afzal Chaudhari
Bus Driver: Mohammad Yunus
Nurse: Maria Da Silva
Shopkeeper: Chandubhai Patel

2 **Cross purposes**
a **vaalaikum assalaam**
b **Thiik hai**
c Rashida
d Bradford **mẽ**
e Leeds **mẽ**
f Headingley Road **par**
g **mãĩ bas mẽ jaatii hũũ**

3 **Nosy parker**
a **aapkaa naam kyaa hai?**
b **aap kahãã rahte hãĩ?**
c **aap kahãã kaam karte hãĩ?**
d **aap kyaa kaam karte hãĩ?**
e **aap vahãã kaise jaate hãĩ?**

4 Here, there and everywhere
a **kahãã**   *b* **kahãã**   *c* **yahãã**   *d* **yahãã**   *e* **kahãã**
f **kahãã**   *g* **vahãã**   *h* **yahãã**   *i* **vahãã**

5 Answering back
a **mãi** Islington **mẽ rahtii hũũ.**
b **mãi Tiichar hũũ.**
c **mãi** Hackney **mẽ kaam kartii hũũ.**
d **mãi kaar mẽ jaatii hũũ.**

6 You and I
a **aap**   *b* **mãi**   *c* **mãi**   *d* **aap**

7 Men and women
a **kartii**   *b* **rahte**   *c* **rahtaa**   *d* **jaatii**   *e* **aate**
f **jaataa**

8 Listening exercise

NAME	JOB	PLACE OF WORK	AREA OF RESIDENCE
Nazir-ul-Haq	Teacher	Handsworth College	Yardley
Tejinder Kaur	Doctor	Ealing	Southall
Dipak Patel	Shopkeeper	Leith Walk	Edinburgh
Jean MacDonald	Lawyer	Liverpool	Ellesmere Port

UNIT 3

Check-ups:
1 Shain's husband, father, and mother
2 Amra and Aneesha
3 Social Worker

1 Cross purposes
a 5, *b* 3, *c* 2, *d* 1, *e* 4, *f*.

2 Starting up
a **sat srii akaal**
b **aap kaisii hãi?**
c **aap kyaa kaam kartii hãi?**
d **aap kahãã kaam kartii hãi?**
e **aapke kitne bachche hãi?**
f **aap kitne bhaaii-bahanẽ hãi?**

3 Family crossword
Across: 1 **bahan**   2 **beTii**   5 **vaalidaa**   6 **bhaaii**   7 **pitaa**
8 **beTaa**
Down: 1 **biivii**   2 **bachche**   3 **vaalid**   4 **maataa**

4 Odd one out
a **bas**
b **vaalid**
c **naam**

5 My, my, my

a **mere**   *b* **merii**   *c* **meraa**   *d* **merii**   *e* **merii**

f **mere**   *g* **mere**   *h* **merii**

6 His and hers

a **inkaa naam** Mr Sardul Singh **hai.**

b **inkaa naam** Mrs Tarsem Kaur **hai.**

c **iskaa naam** Ranjit **hai.**

d **iskaa naam** Bhupinder **hai.**

7 Counting up

a **mere do**   *b* **merii ek**   *c* **mere tiin**   *d* **mere chaar**

e **mere tiin**   *f* **chaar**

8 Listening exercise

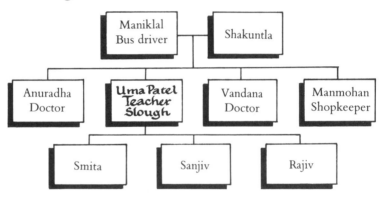

Maniklal
Bus driver

Shakuntla

Anuradha
Doctor

Uma Patel
Teacher
Slough

Vandana
Doctor

Manmohan
Shopkeeper

Smita

Sanjiv

Rajiv

UNIT 4

Check-ups:

1 yoghurt, potatoes, salt

2 In lentil and vegetable dishes

3 No

1 Mixed vegetables

d 3, *a* 6, *g* 5, *c* 2, *e* 1, *f* 4, *b*.

2 Dinner time

a **ye kyaa hai?**

b **methii ko angrezii mē kyaa kahte hãĩ?**

c **isko kyaa karte hãĩ?**

d **isko kyaa kahte hãĩ?**

e **ismē kyaa hai?/ismē kyaa Daalte hãĩ?**

f **kyaa ismē gosht (bhii) hai?**

3 What's in it?

a **dahii, namak, aaluu, garam masaalaa**

b **chaaval, sabzii, ghii, masaale**

c **daal, sabzii, gosht, mirch-masaale**

4   **Word search**
pulaav, chaaval, sabzii, ghii, masaalaa, raaytaa, dahii, aaluu, namak, paalak, methii, daal

5   **Near and far**
a   ye, ye   *b*   is, is   *c*   is   *d*   ye, in   *e*   vo, vo, us, us
f   is, is   *g*   us, us

6   **Questions, questions**
a   kyaa   *b*   kyaa   *c*   kahãã   *d*   kyaa   *e*   kyaa
f   kahãã   *g*   kaise   *h*   kaisii   *i*   kitne   *j*   kitnii

7   **Yes and no**
a   nahĩĩ   *b*   nahĩĩ   *c*   hãã   *d*   hãã   *e*   nahĩĩ
f   nahĩĩ   *g*   hãã   *h*   nahĩĩ   *i*   hãã   *j*   nahĩĩ

8   **Listening exercise**
(kabaab) – gosht, namak, mirch-masaale
(biryaanii) – chaaval, gosht, mirch
(aaluu-gosht) – aaluu, gosht, garam masaalaa

UNIT 5

Check-ups:
1   Four pounds
2   Under the shelf
3   Two

1   **Cross purposes**
c 1, *d* 2, *a* 3, *b* 4, *e* 5.

2   **At the sweet centre**
a   aapko kyaa chaahiye?
b   inko kyaa kahte hãĩ?
c   inkii Kiimat kyaa hai?
d   mujhe ek pleT chaahiye.
e   kyaa aapke paas chaTnii hai?
f   chaTnii kii ek pleT laaiye.

3   **How much is it?**
a   gosht, nabbe   *b*   kaar, pããch hazaar   *c*   mez, tiin sau
d   ghar, pachaas hazaar

4   **What have you got**
a   mere paas   *b*   mere paas   *c*   mere paas   *d*   mere
e   meraa   *f*   merii   *g*   mere paas

5   **What do you want?**
b   mujhe chaaval chaahiyē.
c   mujhe dhaniyaa chaahiye.
d   mujhe aaluu chaahiyē.
e   mujhe ghar chaahiye.
f   mujhe chaar kamre chaahiyē.

g **mujhe kaar chaahiye.**
h **mujhe DaakTar chaahiye.**

6 **Positions**
**mẽ; ke niiche; ke saamne; par; kii; ke paas; kii; ke paas;
ke niiche; ke paas.**

7 **Endings**
**meraa; mere; kamre; chhoTe; kamre; baRaa; kamraa; baRe;
kamre; khiRkiyãã.**

8 **Listening exercise**
Rice should be below veg.
Should be no meat in the fridge.
Should be coriander in front of the shop.
Should be yoghurt in the fridge.

REVIEW 1

A **Saying hello and saying who you are**
1 Names: X Lashkari Ram   Y Gopal Sharma
Religion: Hindu
Health: X Fine   Y Not well

2 Names: P Syeda   Q Zarina
Religion: Muslim
Health: P Fine   Q Fine

B **Talking about yourself**
Jaswant Singh: Lawyer, works in Oxford, lives in Didcot, travels to work by
train.
Robert Coleman: Doctor, works at Radcliffe Hospital, lives on Headington
Rd. in Oxford, drives to work.

C **Introducing a friend to your family**
Amjad: son   Nasreen: younger sister
Asif: younger brother   Parveen: daughter
Shafaq: older brother
Yusuf: father

D **Giving personal and family details**
Name: Devendra Jain
Address: 12 Spencer Rd., Chapeltown, Leeds
Occupation: Unemployed
Number of children: 4
Names: Mahavir, Dharmvir, Shashibala, Archana

E **Getting to know a new friend**
Tarsem: two children, one boy one girl. Son's name Kulwinder, lives in
London, in Richmond, teacher. Daughter Baljinder student in Portsmouth.
One sister living in Ealing.
Usha: One older and one younger brother. Older brother bus driver, living

in Birmingham. Younger brother Indresh also living in Birmingham – shopkeeper. Usha's three daughters – Rita and Anita at secondary school, and Sheela at primary.

F   Preparing a shopping list

Shopping list: garlic, tomatoes, potatoes, spinach, coriander

G   Asking the names of things and their uses

sarsõ   mustard
muulii   radish
pudiinaa   mint
You put **muulii** in salad.

H   Ordering food in a restaurant

One rogan josh, two biriyanis, and one fish and chips.

I   Asking for things at the shop

a   Potatoes, carrots, rice
b   Potatoes – 10p a pound, Carrots – 15p a pound, Rice – 80p a pound.
c   £8.80.

J   Finding your way round the shop

UNIT 6

Check-ups:
1   Waseem
2   He went out (to a wedding)
3   She has a temperature, cough, and a bad throat.
      She's just had a little milk.

1   Aches and pains

b   **mere peT mẽ dard hai.**   *c*   **mujhe sar-dard hai.**
d   **meraa galaa Kharaab hai.**   *e*   **mujhe buKhaar hai.**

2 **Doctor doctor**
(iskii tabiiyat) Kharaab hai/ye Thiik nahĩĩ hai.
isko khããsii hai.
jii nahĩĩ. kal thoRaa saa buKhaar thaa, magar aaj nahĩĩ hai.
iske peT mẽ dard hai.
kal isne pulaav khaayaa.

3 **Go-between**
a aap kaisii hãĩ?
b kyaa baat hai?
c kal aapne kyaa khaayaa?
d kyaa aapko koii aur taKliif bhii hai?
e kyaa aapko sar-dard bhii hai?
f kyaa aapko buKhaar bhii hai?

4 **'Was' or 'were'?**
a thii   b thaa   c thĩĩ   d the   e the   f thaa
g thaa   h thii   i thĩĩ   j thii

5 **kal aapne kyaa khaayaa?**
b pulaav khaayaa   c pakoRe khaae   d dahii khaayaa
e sabziyãã khaaĩĩ   f aaluu khaae

6 **Whither away?**
b Rita, **gaii hãĩ**   c Charan, **gae hãĩ**   d Sunita, **gaii hai**
e Mohan, **gayaa hai**   f Anita, **gaii hai.**

7 **Missing particles**
hii; bhii; to; bhii; hii; saa; sii; bhii.

8 **Listening exercise**
1 Stomach ache, temperature.   2 Cough, sore throat, headache.
3 Temperature, headache.

UNIT 7

Check-ups:
1 No
2 Speaking
3 Yes

1 **Cross purposes**
c 2; b 3; a 4; d 5; e 1.

2 **What do you know?**
a mãĩ hindii siikh rahaa/rahii hũũ.
b mãĩ ek saal se siikh rahaa/rahii hũũ.
c jii? phir kahiye.
d mãĩ nahĩĩ paRh saktaa/saktii, magar apnaa naam likh
saktaa/saktii hũũ.
e mujhe angrezii aatii hai aur thoRii urduu bhii aatii hai.
f maaluum nahĩĩ. aaj mãĩ pahlii dafaa hinduu shaadii mẽ aayaa/aaii
hũũ.

3   Can or can't?

c   nahĩĩ khaa saktaa.   d   nahĩĩ bol saktii.
e   likh saktii hai.   f   nahĩĩ siikh saktaa.
g   nahĩĩ kar saktaa.

4   Action stations

Rajiv **hindii bol rahaa hai.** Bhupinder **khaanaa khaa rahaa hai.** Nazir
hindii kii kitaab paRh rahaa hai. Janice Anita **ko chiTThii likh rahii
hai.** Yvonne **angrezii kii kitaab paRh rahii hai.** Charlie Coca Cola **pii
rahaa hai.** Sean **kaam kar rahaa hai.**

5   Odd one out

a   dost   b   kitaab   c   kal   d   kitaab   e   khaa
f   saktaa hũũ

6   Give and take

c   pii liyaa hai.   d   paRh lii hai.   e   le lii hai.   f   kar dii
hai.   g   de dii hai.   h   kar liyaa hai.

7   mm . . . mm . . . mm . . . mm . . .

mãĩ; mujhe; mãĩne; mãĩ; mujhe; mujhe; meraa; mãĩ; mujhe; mãĩ.

8   Listening exercise

1   Ann Lawson, Teacher. Lives in Rochdale, works in Bolton. Learning
   Urdu for three years, can read and also write a little. Can speak Hindi
   but not read it.
2   Rowshon Malik, lives and works in Tower Hamlets, doctor. Speaks Bengali
   at home, but learning Hindi and Urdu for one year now. Can read and write
   Hindi, but only write name in Urdu.
3   Abdul Rahim. Learnt quite a lot of Urdu at school. Can speak, read, and
   write. Now living in Nottingham, librarian. Learning Hindi for two years.
   Learnt quite a lot, can now also read Hindi books.

UNIT 8

Check-ups:
1   Nazreen Butt
2   Hindi and Urdu films
3   Hot weather

1   Any questions

c 1, d 2, b 3, a 4.

2   Any answers

a   mujhe paRhne kaa shauK hai.
b   mujhe Khaas taur par urduu kii kitaabẽ pasand hãĩ.
c   jii hãã, mujhe hindii siikhne kaa shauK hai.
d   mãĩ do saal se siikh rahii hũũ.
e   bahut achchhii lagtii hai.

3 Pastimes

b khaane   *c* paRhne   *d* sunnaa   *e* gaanaa

f khelnaa   *g* bolne   *h* dekhne

4 What what?

kyaa; kahãã; kaun kaun; kyaa; kyaa; kyaa kyaa; kahãã kahãã; kaun.

5 achchhaa buraa

c dhaniyaa achchhaa lagtaa hai   *d* pakoRe achchhe lagte hãĩ

e sabziyãã burii lagtii hãĩ   *f* methii achchhii lagtii hai

g aaluu achchhe lagte hãĩ   *h* dahii buraa lagtaa hai

6 kyaa/kaun/kis

kyaa; kis; kis; kyaa; kis; kaun; kis.

7 Walkie-talkie

a **kyaa haal-chaal hai?**   How are things?

Thiik-Thaak hai.   Fine.

b **aapke kyaa kyaa shauK hãĩ?**   What are your hobbies?

mujhe khelnaa-kuudnaa pasand   I like sports. I also like going for a

hai. mujhe ghuumne-phirne kaa   stroll.

bhii shauK hai.

c **kyaa aapko urduu yaa hindii aatii**   Do you know Hindi or Urdu?

hai?

bol-chaal kii zabaan aatii hai.   I know the spoken language. I can

baat-chiit kar saktaa hũũ magar   make conversation but I can't read

likh-paRh nahĩĩ saktaa.   and write.

8 Listening exercise

Five for, four against, and one neutral.

UNIT 9

Check-ups:

1 In January

2 Delhi–Jammu: train

Jammu–Srinagar: bus

3 Taj Restaurant

1 Connections

a Cross   *b* Tick   *c* Tick   *d* Tick   *e* Cross

f Cross   *g* Cross   *h* Tick

2 Neighbours

b **aapko kab jaanaa hai?**

c **(aur) (aapko) vaapas kab aanaa hai?**

d **(aapko) vahãã kab jaanaa hai?**

e **(aapko) vahãã kaise jaanaa hai – Tren mẽ yaa bas mẽ?**

f **(aapko) Dundee se vaapas kab aanaa hai?**

g **mujhe afsos hai. kal mujhe London havaaii jahaaz se jaanaa hai.**

3   Shopping list

b   mujhe chaaval Khariidne hãĩ.
c   mujhe paalak Khariidnii hai.
d   mujhe methii Khariidnii hai.
e   mujhe dahii Khariidnaa hai.
f   mujhe aaluu Khariidne hãĩ.
g   mujhe dhaniyaa Khariidnaa hai.

4   Planning the week

Monday **ko mãĩ** Rajiv **ko chiTThii likhnaa chaahtaa/chaahtii hũũ.**
mujhe Anarkali Restaurant **mẽ khaanaa khaanaa hai.**

Tuesday **ko mujhe** London **jaanaa hai. mãĩ kuchh hindii kii kitaabẽ
Khariidnaa chaahtaa/chaahtii hũũ.**

Wednesday **ko mãĩ** badminton **khelnaa chaahtaa/chaahtii hũũ.**
Thursday **ko mãĩ** Bristol **jaanaa chaahtaa/chaahtii hũũ.**
Friday **ko mãĩ tairnaa chaahtaa/chaahtii hũũ. mujhe** cinema **bhii
jaanaa hai.**

5   So what?

a   siikhũũ, sakũũgaa/sakũũgii.
b   banaaẽ, lẽge/lẽgii.
c   dẽ, dũũgaa/dũũgii.
d   chaahẽ, dũũgaa/dũũgii.
e   khaaẽ, hogaa.
f   Daalẽ, lagegaa.
g   gaaũũ, sunegaa/sunegii.
h   bajaaũũ, gaaegii.
i   bolẽ, legaa/legii/lẽge/lẽgii.
j   likhẽ, lagegaa.

6   Time travel

b   kal subah mãĩ London jaaũũgii.
c   kal raat mãĩ Glasgow jaaũũgaa.
d   kal shaam ham Derby jaaẽge.
e   kal dopahar mãĩ Bristol jaaũũgii.
f   kal shaam ham Plymouth jaaẽgii.

7   Yesterday and tomorrow

a   yesterday   b   yesterday   c   tomorrow   d   tomorrow
e   tomorrow   f   yesterday   g   tomorrow

8   Listening exercise

1   Wants to go to India in December by plane, going first to Bombay, and then
    on by train to Madras.
2   Wants to go to Rawalpindi. Will fly to Islamabad and then take bus to
    Rawalpindi. Wants to go in January.
3   Wants two tickets to Kenya, going in November. Will fly to Nairobi, and
    then fly on to Mombassa.

UNIT 10

Check-ups:
1 Her father, mother, and brother.
2 Gorbals Primary, Adelphi Secondary.
3 Community link teacher.
4 After coming to Britain.

1   Personal details

a Tick   *b* Cross   *c* Cross   *d* Cross   *e* Tick
f Cross   *g* Tick   *h* Tick   *i* Cross

2   Go-between

a Where were you born?
b **(ye)** Paris **mẽ paidaa huĩ.**
c Where were you educated?
d **sab se pahle** Paris **mẽ, aur uske baad** London **mẽ.**
e How old were you when you came to London?
f **us vaKt ye das saal kii thĩ.**
g What did you do when you left school?
h Paris **vaapas jaakar inhõne ek saal** department store **mẽ kaam kiyaa.**
i What did you do after that?
j **uske baad ye is mulk mẽ vaapas aaĩ, aur tab se aaj tak ye kaii kaam kar chukii hãĩ.**

3   'Help!'

gae; liye; gaii; chukaa; saktaa; liyaa; gayaa; chukaa; dii; legaa.

4   Getting spliced

b London **jaakar aapne kyaa kiyaa?**
c **vo is mulk mẽ vaapas aakar apnaa kaarobaar shuruu karẽge.**
d **mãĩ urduu siikhkar paakistaan jaanaa chaahtii hũũ.**
e **aapkaa bachchaa ye davaaii lekar Thiik ho jaaegaa.**
f **mãĩne mirch-masaalaa Khariidkar achchhaa khaanaa banaayaa.**
g **ham khaanaa khaakar** television **dekhẽge.**
h **vo kaam karke vaapas gaii.**
i **mãĩ baahar jaakar fuTbaal khelnaa chaahtaa hũũ.**
j **mãĩ thoRii hindii siikhkar hindustaanii dostõ ke saath baat-chiit kar saktii hũũ.**

5   A question of relativity

a **k**   *b* **k**   *c* **j**   *d* **j**   *e* **k**   *f* **k**   *g* **j**   *h* **k**   *i* **j**

a **aapkaa naam** *kyaa* **hai?**
b **aap** *kahãã* **rahte/rahtii hãĩ?**
c **mãĩ vahãã rahtaa/rahtii hũũ** *jahãã* **aap kaam karte/kartii hãĩ.**
d *jab* **aap yahãã aae/aaĩ, tab aapkii umr kitnii thii?**
e **jab aap vaapas gae/gaĩ, tab aapkii umr** *kitnii* **thii?**
f **aapko** *kis* **Kism kaa khaanaa pasand hai?**
g **mujhe vo khaanaa pasand hai** *jismẽ* **masaale bahut hõ.**
h **aapko** *kaun sii* **filmẽ pasand hãĩ?**
i **kyaa aapko vo sangiit pasand hai** *jo* **filmõ mẽ bajaate hãĩ?**

6 **Passive agreement**
a 4, *b* 3, *c* 3, *d* 1, *e* 5, *f* 8, *g* 5, *h* 6.

7 **The teacher's story**
c, f, b, g, e, a, d.

8 **Listening exercise**
Name: Jay Prakash
Address: 10, High St., Preston
Education: Salwan Boys' Upper Secondary School, New Delhi.
Work Experience: machine operator, bus driver, shopkeeper.

Name: Vijay Singh
Address: 92, Manchester Rd., Blackburn
Education: N/A
Work Experience: Various restaurants.

Name: Feroze Khan
Address: 297 Stratford Rd., Birmingham
Education: Steward's Centre
Work Experience: Waiter, taxi driver, restaurateur.

Word groups

In this section, words are grouped according to areas of meaning under the following topic headings:

1 Numbers
2 Hours, days, months
3 Foods, drinks and tastes
4 Clothes
5 Colours
6 Around the house
7 Transport and travel
8 Spare time
9 The family
10 The body, health and ailments

A 'p' in brackets along with 'm' or 'f' indicates plural.

1 Numbers

Cardinal numbers

1	ek	11	gyaaraa	21	ikkiis
2	do	12	baaraa	22	baaiis
3	tiin	13	teraa	23	teiis
4	chaar	14	chaudaa	24	chaubiis
5	pããch	15	pandraa	25	pachchiis
6	chhe	16	solaa	26	chhabbiis
7	saat	17	sattraa	27	sattaaiis
8	aaTh	18	aThaaraa	28	aTThaaiis
9	nau	19	unniis	29	untiis
10	das	20	biis	30	tiis

31	iktiis	41	iktaaliis	51	ikyaavan
32	battiis	42	bayaaliis	52	baavan
33	tãĩtiis	43	tẽtaaliis	53	tirpan
34	chaũtiis	44	chauvaaliis	54	chauvan
35	paĩtiis	45	paĩtaaliis	55	pachpan
36	chhattiis	46	chhiyaaliis	56	chhappan
37	saĩtiis	47	saĩtaaliis	57	sattaavan
38	aRtiis	48	aRtaaliis	58	aTThaavan
39	untaaliis	49	unchaas	59	unsaTh
40	chaaliis	50	pachaas	60	saaTh

61	iksaTh	71	ikahattar	81	ikyaasii
62	baasaTh	72	bahattar	82	bayaasii
63	tirsaTh	73	tihattar	83	tiraasii
64	chaũsaTh	74	chauhattar	84	chauraasii
65	paĩsaTh	75	pachahattar	85	pachaasii
66	chhiyaasaTh	76	chhihattar	86	chhiyaasii
67	saRsaTh	77	satahattar	87	sataasii
68	aRsaTh	78	aThahattar	88	aThaasii
69	unhattar	79	unaasii	89	navaasii
70	sattar	80	assii	90	nabbe

91	ikyaanabe	101	ek sau ek
92	baanabe	102	ek sau do
93	tiraanabe		
94	chauraanabe	200	do sau
95	panchaanabe	300	tiin sau
96	chhiyaanabe		
97	sattanabe	420	chaar sau biis
98	aTThaanabe	777	saat sau satahattar
99	ninyaanabe		
100	(ek) sau	1,000	(ek) hazaar

1,001	ek hazaar ek
2,000	do hazaar
3,000	tiin hazaar
10,000	das hazaar
10,456	das hazaar chaar sau chhappan
100,000	ek laakh
1,000,000	das laakh
10,000,000	ek karoR

Ordinal numbers

first	**pahlaa**	sixth	**chhaThaa**
second	**duusraa**	seventh	**saatvãã**
third	**tiisraa**	eighth	**aaThvãã**
fourth	**chauthaa**	ninth	**nauvãã**
fifth	**pããchvãã**	tenth	**dasvãã**

2 Hours, days, months

Hours

One o'clock	ek bajaa
at one o'clock	ek baje
two o'clock	do baje
at two o'clock	do baje
three o'clock	tiin baje
etc	

quarter to eleven	paune gyaaraa (baje)
quarter past eight	savaa aaTh (baje)
half past six	saaRhe chhe (baje)
etc	

Note these special forms

quarter to one	paunaa bajaa
at quarter to one	paune baje
quarter past one	savaa bajaa
at quarter past one	savaa baje
half past one	DeRh bajaa
at half past one	DeRh baje
(at) half past two	Dhaaii baje

ten minutes past three	tiin bajkar das minaT
ten to three	tiin bajne mẽ das minaT
etc	

Days of the week

English	Hindi	Urdu
Sunday	ravivaar/itvaar	itvaar
Monday	somvaar	somvaar, piir
Tuesday	mangalvaar	mangalvaar
Wednesday	budhvaar	budhvaar
Thursday	guruvaar/viirvaar	jumaaraat,
	brahaspativaar	jumeraat
Friday	shukravaar	jumaa
Saturday	shanivaar	haftaa
	shaniicharvaar	saniicharvaar

Months

January	janvarii	July	julaaii
February	farvarii	August	agast
March	maarch	September	sitambar
April	aprail	October	aktuubar
May	maii	November	navambar
June	juun	December	disambar

3 Foods, drinks and tastes

Foodgrains and flours

chickpea flour (gram flour)	**besan** (m)
chickpeas	**chane** (m p)
corn	**makaii** (f)
flour	**aaTaa** (m)
flour (fine)	**maidaa** (m)
lentils	**daal** (f s)
rice	**chaaval** (m p)
wheat	**gandam, gehũ** (f s)

Vegetables

aubergine	**bãĩgan** (m)
bitter gourd	**karelaa** (m)
cabbage	**band gobhii** (f)
carrot	**gaajar** (f)
cauliflower	**gobhii** (f)
corn on the cob	**bhuTTaa** (m)
fenugreek	**methii** (f)
marrow	**laukii** (f)
mustard (leaves)	**sarsõ** (f)
okra	**bhinDii** (f)
onion	**pyaaz** (m)
peas	**maTar** (m p)
potato	**aaluu** (m)
pumpkin	**kadduu** (m)
radish	**muulii** (f)
spinach	**paalak** (f)
tomato	**TamaaTar** (m)
vegetable	**sabzii** (f)

Herbs and spices

black cardamom	**baRii ilaaychii** (f)
black pepper	**kaalii mirch** (f)
chilli	**mirch** (f)
cinnamon	**daalchiinii** (f)
cloves	**laung** (m)
coriander	**dhaniyaa** (m)
cumin	**jiiraa** (m)
garlic	**lahsun, thom** (m)
ginger (dry)	**sõTh** (f)
ginger (fresh)	**adrak** (m)
green cardamom	**chhoTii ilaaychii** (f)
mango powder	**amchuur** (m)
mint	**pudiinaa** (m)
mixed spices	**garam masaalaa** (m)
mustard (seeds)	**raaii** (f)

salt	**namak** (m)
tamarind	**imlii** (f)
turmeric	**haldii** (f)

Fruits and nuts

almond	**baadaam** (m)
apple	**seb** (m)
banana	**kelaa** (m)
fruit	**phal** (m)
grapes	**anguur** (m)
guava	**amruud** (m)
lemon	**niimbuu** (m)
mango	**aam** (m)
melon	**Kharbuuzaa** (m)
orange	**santaraa** (m)
peach	**aaRuu** (m)
peanuts	**mũũgphalii** (f)
pear	**naashpaatii** (f)
pistachio	**pistaa** (m)
plum	**aaluubuKhaaraa** (m)
tangerine	**naarangii** (f)
walnut	**akhroT** (m)
watermelon	**tarbuuz** (m)

Miscellaneous

alchoholic drink	**sharaab** (f)
betel leaf	**paan** (m)
bread	**roTii** (f)
breads, Indian	**naan** (m), **chapaatii** (f), **puuRii** (f), **paraaThaa** (m)
butter	**makkhan** (m)
cigarette	**sigreT** (f)
coffee	**kaafii** (f)
cooked rice	**bhaat** (m)
curry	**saalan** (m)
egg	**anDaa** (m)
juice	**ras** (m)
meat	**gosht** (m)
milk	**duudh** (m)
oil	**tel** (m)
clarified butter	**ghii** (m)
sugar	**chiinii, shakkar** (f)
tea	**chaay** (f)
tobacco	**tambaakuu** (m)
water	**paanii** (m)
yoghurt	**dahii** (m)

Tastes

bitter	**kaRvaa**
delicious	**svaadishTh** (Hindi), **Khushzaaykaa** (Urdu)
savoury	**namkiin**
sour	**khaTTaa**
spicy	**masaaledaar, chaTpaTaa**
sweet	**miiThaa**
tasty	**mazedaar**

4   Clothes

dress (clothing)	**kapRe** (m)
glasses	**chashmaa** (m), **ainak** (f)
gloves	**dastaane** (m p)
hat	**Topii** (f)
kurta	**kurtaa** (m)
pyjamas	**paayjaamaa/paajaamaa** (m)
sari	**saaRii** (f)
scarf	**dupaTTa** (m)
shalwar	**shalvaar** (f)
shirt	**Kamiiz** (f)
shoes	**juutaa** (m)
socks	**juraabẽ** (f p)
trousers	**patluun** (f)
turban	**pagRii** (f), **dastaar** (f) (Urdu)
umbrella	**chhaataa** (m)

5   Colours

black	**kaalaa**
blue	**niilaa**
brown	**bhuuraa**
colour	**rang**
green	**haraa, sabz** (Urdu)
orange	**naarangii**
pink	**gulaabii**
purple	**bãĩganii**
red	**laal, surKh** (Urdu)
white	**safed**
white (skin)	**goraa**
yellow	**piilaa, zard** (Urdu)

6   Around the house

bathroom	**Gusal-Khaanaa** (m)
carpet	**darii** (f), **Kaaliin** (m)
chair	**kursii** (f)
cup	**kap** (m), **pyaalii** (f)

dining table	**khaane kii mez** (f)
door	**darvaazaa** (m)
floor	**farsh** (m)
glass	**gilaas** (m)
house	**ghar, makaan** (m)
kitchen	**rasoiighar** (m) (Hindi), **baavarchii-Khaanaa** (m) (Urdu)
knife	**chaaKuu** (m), **chhurii** (f)
ladle	**karchhi, kalchhii** (f)
plate	**pleT** (f)
platter	**thaalii** (f)
pot	**bartan** (m)
roof, ceiling	**chhat** (f)
room	**kamraa** (m)
saucepan (large)	**patiilaa** (m)
saucepan (small)	**patiilii** (f)
soap	**saabun** (m)
spoon	**chammach** (m)
table	**mez** (f)
teapot	**chaaydaanii** (f)
towel	**tauliyaa** (m)
window	**khiRkii** (f)
wok	**kaRaaii** (f)

7 Transport and travel

aeroplane	**havaaii jahaaz** (m)
airport	**havaaii aDDaa** (m)
bicycle	**saaiikil** (f)
bus	**bas** (f)
car	**kaar** (f)
fare	**kiraayaa** (m)
journey	**safar** (m), **yaatraa** (f) (Hindi)
passenger	**savaarii** (f)
return ticket	**vaapasii kii TikaT**
rickshaw	**rikshaa** (f)
ship	**samundarii jahaaz** (m)
single ticket	**ek tarfaa TikaT**
ticket	**TikaT** (f)
train	**Tren** (f), **rel gaaRii** (f)
vehicle	**gaaRii** (f)

8 Spare time

book	**kitaab** (f)
cooking	**khaanaa pakaanaa** (m), **khaanaa banaanaa** (m)
dancing	**naachnaa** (m)
gardening	**baaGvaanii** (f)

hobby	**shauK** (m)
music	**sangiit** (m) (Hindi), **muusiiKii** (f) (Urdu)
newspaper	**aKhbaar** (m)
playing (music)	**bajaanaa** (m)
playing (sport)	**khelnaa** (m)
reading	**paRhnaa** (m)
song, singing	**gaanaa** (m)
swimming	**tairnaa** (m)
walking	**ghuumnaa-phirnaa** (m)

9   The family

brother	**bhaaii**
child (female)	**bachchii**
child (male)	**bachchaa**
daughter	**beTii**
daughter-in-law	**bahuu**
daughter's daughter	**naatin**
daughter's son	**naatii**
father	**pitaa** (Hindi), **vaalid** (Urdu), **abbaa** (Urdu), **baap**
father-in-law	**sasur, susar**
father's older brother	**taayaa, taauu**
father's sister	**phuuphii, buaa**
father's younger brother	**chaachaa** (Hindi), **chachaa** (Urdu)
husband	**pati** (Hindi), **Khaavind** (Urdu), **shauhar** (Urdu)
maternal grandfather	**naanaa**
maternal grandmother	**naanii**
mother	**maataa** (Hindi), **vaalidaa** (Urdu), **mā̃a**
mother-in-law	**saas**
mother's brother	**maamaa** (Hindi), **maamuu** (Urdu)
mother's sister	**mausii** (Hindi), **Khaalaa** (Urdu)
paternal grandfather	**daadaa**
paternal grandmother	**daadii**
relative	**sambandhii** (Hindi), **rishtedaar** (Urdu)
sister	**bahan**
son	**beTaa**
son-in-law	**daamaad**
son's daughter	**potii**
son's son	**potaa**
wife	**patnii** (Hindi), **biivii** (Urdu)

10 The body, health and ailments

Parts of the body

arm	**bãah** (f), **baazuu** (m) (Urdu)
back	**piiTh** (f)
bald	**ganjaa**
blood	**lahu** (m), **Khuun** (m)
body	**shariir** (m) (Hindi), **jism** (m) (Urdu)
chest	**chhaatii** (f)
ear	**kaan** (m)
elbow	**kuhnii** (f)
eye	**ãakh** (f)
face	**chehraa** (m)
finger	**ungal, ungalii** (f)
foot	**pair** (m), **pãav** (m)
hair	**baal** (m)
hand	**haath** (m)
head	**sir** (m) (Hindi), **sar** (m) (Urdu)
heart	**dil** (m)
knee	**ghuTnaa** (m)
leg	**laat** (f)
lip	**hõTh** (m), **lab** (m) (Urdu)
mouth	**mũũh** (m)
neck	**gardan** (f)
nose	**naak** (m)
shoulder	**kandhaa** (m)
stomach	**peT** (m)
throat	**galaa** (m)
thumb	**anguuThaa** (m)
toe	**pair kii ungalii** (f)
tongue	**jiibh** (f), **zabaan** (f) (Urdu)
tooth	**dãat** (m)

Health and ailments

blind	**andhaa**
breath	**sãas** (f)
common cold	**zukaam** (m)
cough	**khãasii** (f)
deaf	**bahraa**
dumb	**gũũgaa**
elderly	**buzurg**
headache	**sar-dard, sir-dard** (m)
health	**tabiiyat** (f)
healthy	**svasth** (Hindi), **sehatmand** (Urdu), **tandrust**
high temperature	**buKhaar** (m)
ill	**biimaar**

injury	**choT** (f)
lame	**langaRaa**
pain, ache	**dard** (m)
patient	**mariiz** (m), **biimaar** (m)
rash	**Khaarish** (f)
sprain	**moch** (f)
wound	**zaKhm** (m)
wounded	**zaKhmii**

Vocabulary

Notes

1. The English translations given here are appropriate for the words as they are used in this course.
2. The words are entered in English alphabetical order ignoring the presence or absence of ~ or ˇ and the distinction between small and capital letters.
3. Some irregular and oblique forms are entered if they have appeared in the dialogues, but all verbs are given in their stem form and adjectives in the masculine singular form.
4. Most of the words taught in this course are used in both Hindi and Urdu. Some, however, are normally restricted to only one of the languages. These are marked with (Hindi) or (Urdu) in brackets.
5. The following abbreviations are used:
   m   masculine noun
   f   feminine noun
   adj   adjective
   adv   adverb

A

aa   come
aaj   today
aaluu (m)   potato
aap   you (polite)
aapkaa (adj)   your (polite)
aaTh   eight
ab   now
achchhaa (adj)   good
achchhaa!   'I see!'/'Well!'

agar   if
aise (adv)   thus
(ke) andar   inside
angrezii (f)   English (language)
angrezii (adj)   English
apnaa (adj)   my, your, his, her, . . .
assalaam alaikum   Muslim greeting
aThaaraa   eighteen
aur   and, in addition, else

B

(ke) baad after (in time)
baahar out, outside
baat (f) matter, thing
bachchaa (m) child
bahan (f) sister
bahut very, much, more
baiTh sit
bajaa play (instrument)
ban become
banaa make
baRaa (adj) big, older
bas (f) bus
bech sell
beTaa (m) son
beTii (f) daughter
bhaaii (m) brother
bhaashaa (f) (Hindi) language
bhar pay
bhii also
(ke) biich (mẽ) between
biivii (f) (Urdu) wife
bol speak
buKhaar (m) temperature
buraa (adj) bad

C

chaah want
chaahiye desirable, required
chaaliis forty
chaar four
chaaval (m) rice
chaay (f) tea
chhe six
chhoTaa (adj) small, younger
chiTThii (f) letter
chuk (helping verb) 'complete'

D

daadaa paternal grandfather
DaakTar (m f) doctor
Daal put
daal (f) lentils
dafaa (f) time
dahii (m) yoghurt
dard (m) pain
das ten
davaaii (f) medicine

de give
dekh see
desh (m) (Hindi) country
dhaniyaa (m) coriander
dhanyavaad (Hindi) 'thank you'
dillii (f) Delhi
do two
donõ both
dopahar (m) afternoon
dost (m f) friend
Draaiivar (m f) driver
dukaan (f) shop
dukaandaar (m f) shopkeeper
duudh (m) milk

E

ek one

F

farvarii (m) February
fuTbaal (m) football

G

gaa sing
gaajar (f) carrot
gaanaa (m) song
galaa (m) throat
garam (adj) hot
garmii (f) heat
gayaa -aa form of **jaa**
Gazal (f) ghazal
ghii (m) ghee
ghuumnaa-phirnaa (m) walking, strolling
giTaar (m) guitar
gosht (m) meat

H

hãã yes
haal (m) condition
hai is
hãĩ are
ham we
hamaaraa (adj) our
hamẽ to us
havaaii jahaaz (m) aeroplane
hii only
hindustaanii (adj) Indian
ho become, happen

huaa -aa form of **ho**
hũũ am

I

inkaa (adj) his, her, their
is oblique form of **ye/yah**
iskaa (adj) his, her, its

J

jaa go
jaan know
jab when
jahãã where
jaisaa (adj) as
janvarii (m) January
jii marker of respect
jis oblique form of **jo**
jitnaa (adj) as much
jo which

K

kaa of
kaafii (adj) much, quite
kaam (m) work
kaar (f) car
kaarobaar (m) business
kab when?
kabaab (m) kebab
kah say, call
kahãã where?
kaii several
kaisaa (adj) how?
kaise (adv) how?
kal yesterday, tomorrow
kam (adj) little, less
kamraa (m) room
kar do
kaun who?
khaa eat
khaanaa (m) food
Khaas taur par especially
khããsii (f) cough
Khaavind (m) (Urdu) husband
Kharaab (adj) bad, sore
Khariid buy
Khayaal (m) opinion
khel play
khiRkii (f) window

Kiimat (f) price
kis oblique form of **kyaa, kaun**
Kism (f) type
kitaab (f) book
kitnaa (adj) how much?
kiyaa -aa form of **kar**
klaas (f) class
klaasiikii muusiiKii (f) classical music
ko to
koii any, some
kuchh some
kursii (f) chair
kyaa what? also a marker of 'yes/no' question

L

laa bring
lag attach, strike, seem
lahsun (m) garlic
landan London
le take
liijiye 'please take'
likh write
(ke) liye for

M

maaluum (adj) known
maataa (f) (Hindi) mother
magar but
mãĩ I
masaalaa (m) spice
mausam (m) weather, season
mẽ in
meharbaanii (f) kindness
mehnat (f) hard work
meraa (adj) my
methii (f) fenugreek
mez (f) table
milkar baRii Khushii huii 'pleased to meet you'
mirch (f) chilli
mujhe to me
mujhe afsos hai 'I am sorry'
mulk (m) (Urdu) country
muulii (f) radish

N

na   used as a tag question
naam (m)   name
nahĩĩ   no, not
namak (m)   salt
namaste   Hindu greeting
nambar (m)   mark, number
nars (m f)   nurse
ne   'special agent' postposition
(ke) niiche   under, beneath

P

pããch   five
paalak (f)   spinach
(ke) paas   near
paaunD (m)   pound
pahlaa (adj)   first
(se) pahle   before (in time)
paidaa   born
pakaa   cook
pakoRaa (m)   pakora
par   on
paRh   read
paRhaa   teach
paRhaaii (f)   studies
parsõ   day after tomorrow, day before
    yesterday
pasand (adj)   likeable
pati (m) (Hindi)   husband
patnii (f) (Hindi)   wife
peT (m)   stomach
phir   again, then
pii   drink
(ke) piichhe   behind
pitaa (m) (Hindi)   father
pleT (f)   plate
prograam (m)   programme
pudiinaa (m)   mint
pulaav (m)   pilao
pyaaz (m)   onion

R

raah (f)   way, path
raat (f)   night
raaytaa (m)   raita
rah   stay, live
rahaa   (helping verb) 'ongoing'
rakh   place

S

saa   '-ish'
saahab (m)   Mr, marker of respect
saal (m)   year
(ke) saamne   in front of, opposite
(ke) saath   with
(ke) saath-saath   along with
sab   all
sabzii (f)   vegetable
safar (m)   journey
sak   (helping verb) 'can'
sangiit (m)   music
sar-dard (m)   headache
sardii (f)   cold
sarsõ (f)   mustard
sat srii akaal   Sikh greeting
shaadii (f)   wedding
shaam (f)   evening
sharaab (f)   alchoholic drink
shauK (m)   hobby, interest
shukriyaa (Urdu)   'thank you'
shuruu   beginning
siikh   learn
sikhaa   teach
sitaar (m)   sitar
subah (f)   morning
sun   hear, listen to

T

tab   then
tabiiyat (f)   health
tair   swim
tak   up to
taKliif (f)   trouble, difficulty
TamaaTar (m)   tomato
tashriif rakhiye (Urdu)   'please sit down'
thaa   past tense of **hai**
Thiik   fine
thoRaa   a little
Tiichar (m f)   teacher
tiin   three
TikaT (f)   ticket
to   'as for', then
Tren (f)   train
tum   you (familiar)
tumhaaraa (adj)   your
tuu   you (very familiar)

U

umr (f)   age
un   oblique form of **vo/ve**
unhône   they (special agent)
unkaa (adj)   his, her, their
us   oblique form of **vo/vah**
utnaa (adj)   so much
(ke) uupar   on, above

V

vaalaikum assalaam   reply to **assalaam alaikum**
vaalid (m) (Urdu)   father
vaalidaa (f) (Urdu)   mother
vaapas (adv)   back
vaGairaa   etcetera
vah (Hindi)   that, he, she, it
vahāā   there
vaisaa (adj)   such
vakiil (m f)   lawyer
vaKt (m)   time
ve (Hindi)   those, they
vesh (m) (Hindi)   dress, clothing
vo   that, those, he, she, it, they

Y

yaa   or
yaad (f)   memory
yah (Hindi)   this, he, she, it
yahāā   here
ye   this, these, he, she, it, they

Z

zabaan (f) (Urdu)   language
zyaadaa (adj)   many, much, more, excessive

Listening exercises
-Transcripts

UNIT 1

1   **assalaam alaikum.**

2   **vaalaikum assalaam.**

1   **meraa naam** Imran Khan **hai. aapkaa naam kyaa hai?**

2   **meraa naam** Muhammad Ali **hai. aap kaise hãĩ?**

1   **mãĩ Thiik hũũ. aap kaise hãĩ?**

2   **mãĩ bhii Thiik hũũ.**

UNIT 2

Sneh:	**aapkaa naam kyaa hai?**
Nazir-ul-Haq:	Nazir-ul-Haq.
Sneh:	**aap kyaa kaam karte hãĩ?**
Nazir-ul-Haq:	**mãĩ Tiichar hũũ.**
Sneh:	**aap kahãã kaam karte hãĩ?**
Nazir-ul-Haq:	**mãĩ** Handsworth College **mẽ kaam kartaa hũũ.**
Sneh:	**aap kahãã rahte hãĩ?**
Nazir-ul-Haq:	Yardley **mẽ.**

Sneh:	**meraa naam** Sneh Gupta **hai. aapkaa naam kyaa hai?**
Tejinder:	**meraa naam** Tejinder Kaur (**tejindar kaur**) **hai.**
Sneh:	**aap kahãã rahtii hãĩ?**
Tejinder:	**mãĩ** Southall **mẽ rahtii hũũ.**
Sneh:	**aap kyaa kaam kartii hãĩ?**
Tejinder:	**mãĩ DaakTar hũũ.**
Sneh:	**aap kahãã kaam kartii hãĩ?**
Tejinder:	Ealing **mẽ.**

Sneh:	**namaste.**
Dipak:	**namaste.**
Sneh:	**meraa naam** Sneh Gupta **hai. aapkaa naam kyaa hai?**
Dipak:	Dipak Patel (**diipak paTel**).

Sneh:	aap kahãã rahte hãĩ, Dipak?
Dipak:	Edinburgh mẽ.
Sneh:	Edinburgh mẽ aap kahãã kaam karte hãĩ?
Dipak:	Leith Walk par.
Sneh:	vahãã aap kyaa kaam karte hãĩ?
Dipak:	mãĩ vahãã dukaandaar hũũ.

Sneh:	aapkaa naam kyaa hai?
Jean:	meraa naam Jean MacDonald hai.
Sneh:	aap kyaa kaam kartii hãĩ, Jean?
Jean:	mãĩ Liverpool mẽ vakiil hũũ.
Sneh:	aap kahãã rahtii hãĩ?
Jean:	mãĩ Ellesmere Port mẽ rahtii hũũ.

UNIT 3

Uma:	ye merii maataa jii hãĩ. inkaa naam Shakuntla hai. aur ye mere pitaa jii hãĩ. inkaa naam Maniklal hai.
Harbans:	aapke pitaa jii kyaa kaam karte hãĩ?
Uma:	Bus driver hãĩ.
Harbans:	achchhaa, aur ye kaun hãĩ?
Uma:	ye merii baRii bahan hãĩ. ye DaakTar hãĩ.
Harbans:	inkaa naam kyaa hai?
Uma:	Anuradha. aur merii chhoTii bahan kaa naam Vandana hai. ye bhii DaakTar hai.
Harbans:	aur ye kaun hãĩ?
Uma:	ye meraa bhaaii hai. iskaa naam Manmohan hai.
Harbans:	ye kyaa kaam karte hãĩ?
Uma:	ye dukaandaar hai.
Harbans:	aapke kitne bachche hãĩ?
Uma:	hamaare tiin bachche hãĩ. ye merii beTii hai. iskaa naam Smita hai. aur ye mere do beTe hãĩ. iskaa naam Sanjiv hai aur iskaa naam Rajiv hai.

UNIT 4

Peter:	ye kyaa hai?
Omar:	isko kabaab kahte hãĩ.
Peter:	achchhaa, kabaab. ismẽ kyaa hai?
Omar:	ismẽ gosht, namak aur mirch-masaale hãĩ.

Peter:	aur isko kyaa kahte hãĩ?
Omar:	ye biryaanii hai. ismẽ chaaval aur gosht hãĩ.
Peter:	kyaa ismẽ sabziyãã bhii hãĩ?
Omar:	jii nahĩĩ, ismẽ sabziyãã nahĩĩ hãĩ.
Peter:	kyaa ismẽ mirch hai?
Omar:	jii hãã, hai.

Peter:	usko kyaa kahte hãĩ?
Omar:	vo aaluu-gosht hai.
Peter:	achchhaa, aaluu-gosht. kyaa usmẽ aaluu aur gosht hãĩ?

Omar: jii hā̃ā, hā̃ī.
Peter: kyaa usmē garam masaalaa bhii Daalte hā̃ī?
Omar: jii, Daalte hā̃ī.

UNIT 5

Sandra: namaste.
Rama: namaste.
Sandra: kyaa aapke paas chaaval hā̃ī?
Rama: jii hā̃ā, hā̃ī.
Sandra: kahā̃ā hā̃ī?
Rama: aapke saamne hā̃ī, sabziyō ke niiche.
Sandra: achchhaa, mujhe aaluu bhii chaahiyē.
Rama: aaluu bhii sabziyō ke niiche hā̃ī. aapko aur kyaa chaahiye?
Sandra: mujhe gosht bhii chaahiye.
Rama: hamaare paas gosht nahī̃ī hai.
Sandra: achchhaa . . . aur kyaa? . . . coriander – **hindii mē** coriander **ko kyaa kahte hā̃ī?**
Rama: coriander **ko dhaniyaa kahte hā̃ī. kyaa aapko dhaniyaa bhii chaahiye?**
Sandra: jii hā̃ā. kahā̃ā hai?
Rama: vo baahar hai, dukaan ke saamne.
Sandra: achchhaa, dhanyavaad. kyaa aapke paas dahii bhii hai?
Rama: jii hā̃ā, dahii fridge mē hai.
Sandra: fridge **kahā̃ā hai?**
Rama: yahā̃ā, mirch-masaalō ke niiche.

Review 1

A

Lashkari Ram: namaste.
Gopal Sharma: namaste.
Lashkari Ram: **meraa naam** Lashkari Ram **hai.**
Gopal Sharma: achchhaa, milkar baRii Khushii huii. meraa naam Gopal Sharma hai. aap kaise hā̃ī?
Lashkari Ram: mā̃ī Thiik hū̃ū. aap kaise hā̃ī?
Gopal Sharma: aaj mā̃ī Thiik nahī̃ī hū̃ū.

Syeda Begum: assalaam alaikum.
Zarina Chaudry: vaalaikum assalaam.
Syeda Begum: aapkaa naam kyaa hai?
Zarina Chaudry: Zarina Chaudry.
Syeda Begum: **meraa naam** Syeda **hai. aap kaisii hā̃ī?**
Zarina Chaudry: mā̃ī Thiik hū̃ū, shukriyaa. aapkaa kyaa haal hai?
Syeda Begum: **Thiik hai, shukriyaa . . . achchhaa, aapse milkar baRii Khushii huii. Khudaa haafiz.**
Zarina Chaudry: **Khudaa haafiz.**

B

Jaswant Singh:	**meraa naam** Jaswant Singh **hai.**
Robert Coleman:	**milkar baRii Khushii huii. meraa naam** Robert Coleman **hai. aap kyaa kaam karte hãĩ?**
Jaswant Singh:	**mãĩ vakiil hũũ.**
Robert Coleman:	**achchhaa? aap kahãã kaam karte hãĩ?**
Jaswant Singh:	**yahãã,** Oxford **mẽ.**
Robert Coleman:	**kyaa aap** Oxford **mẽ rahte bhii hãĩ?**
Jaswant Singh:	**jii nahĩĩ, mãĩ** Didcot **mẽ rahtaa hũũ. aap kyaa kaam karte hãĩ?**
Robert Coleman:	**mãĩ DaakTar hũũ. mãĩ** Radcliffe Hospital **mẽ kaam kartaa hũũ.**
Jaswant Singh:	**aap kahãã rahte hãĩ?**
Robert Coleman:	**yahãã,** Oxford **mẽ.**
Jaswant Singh:	**achchhaa,** Oxford **mẽ kahãã?**
Robert Coleman:	Headington Rd **par.**
Jaswant Singh:	**achchhaa, vahãã. vahãã se aap** Hospital **kaise jaate hãĩ?**
Robert Coleman:	**kaar mẽ. aap** Didcot **se yahãã kaise aate hãĩ?**
Jaswant Singh:	**mãĩ Tren mẽ aataa hũũ.**

C

Parvez:	**ye meraa chhoTaa bhaaii hai. iskaa naam** Asif **hai.**
Martin:	Hello, Asif.
Asif:	Hello.
Parvez:	**aur ye mere baRe bhaaii hãĩ. inkaa naam** Shafaq **hai.**
Martin:	**assalaam alaikum.**
Shafaq:	**vaalaikum assalaam.**
Parvez:	**ye mere vaalid hãĩ.**
Martin:	**aapse milkar baRii Khushii huii.**
Father:	**bahut meharbaanii.**
Parvez:	**aur ye merii chhoTii bahan** Nasreen **hai.**
Martin:	**assalaam alaikum.**
Nasreen:	**vaalaikum assalaam.**
Martin:	**aur ye kaun hãĩ** Parvez **saahab?**
Parvez:	**ye? ye mere bachche hãĩ. ye meraa beTaa hai. iskaa naam** Amjad **hai.**
Martin:	**aur ye?**
Parvez:	**ye merii beTii hai.**
Martin:	Hello. **aapkaa naam kyaa hai?**
Parveen:	**meraa naam** Parveen **hai. aapkaa naam kyaa hai?**

D

Baljit Kaur:	**aapkaa naam kyaa hai?**
Devendra Jain:	**meraa naam** Devendra Jain **hai.**
Baljit Kaur:	**aap kahãã rahte hãĩ?**
Devendra Jain:	Leeds **mẽ.**
Baljit Kaur:	Leeds **mẽ kahãã?**
Devendra Jain:	Chapeltown **mẽ,** 12 Spencer Rd **par.**
Baljit Kaur:	**aap kyaa kaam karte hãĩ?**
Devendra Jain:	**mãĩ kaam nahĩĩ kartaa.**
Baljit Kaur:	**aapke kitne bachche hãĩ?**

Devendra Jain:	**mere chaar bachche hãĩ.**
Baljit Kaur:	**achchhaa? kitne beTe, aur kitnii beTiyãã?**
Devendra Jain:	**do beTe, do beTiyãã.**
Baljit Kaur:	**beTõ ke naam kyaa hãĩ?**
Devendra Jain:	**baRe beTe kaa naam** Mahavir **hai aur chhoTe kaa naam** Dharmvir **hai.**
Baljit Kaur:	**aur beTiyõ ke naam?**
Devendra Jain:	**baRii beTii kaa naam** Shashibala **hai, aur chhoTii kaa naam** Archana **hai.**
Baljit Kaur:	**shukriyaa.**

E

Usha Sharma:	**aapke kitne bachche hãĩ?**
Tarsem Kaur:	**hamaare do bachche hãĩ, ek beTaa aur ek beTii.**
Usha:	**achchhaa? beTe kaa naam kyaa hai?**
Tarsem:	Kulwinder. **vo** London **mẽ rahtaa hai.**
Usha:	London **mẽ kahãã?**
Tarsem:	Richmond **mẽ. vo Tiichar hai.**
Usha:	**bahut achchhaa. kyaa aapkii beTii bhii vahãã rahtii hai?**
Tarsem:	**jii nahĩĩ. merii beTii** Portsmouth **mẽ hai. uskaa naam** Baljinder **hai. vo** student **hai.**
Usha:	**aur aap kitne bhaaii-bahanẽ hãĩ?**
Tarsem:	**ham do hii hãĩ. mãĩ aur merii bahan.**
Usha:	**achchhaa? aapkii bahan kahãã rahtii hai?**
Tarsem:	Ealing **mẽ. aap kitne bhaaii-bahanẽ hãĩ?**
Usha:	**ham tiin hãĩ. mãĩ, ek baRe bhaaii, aur ek chhoTaa bhaaii.**
Tarsem:	**baRe bhaaii saahab kyaa kaam karte hãĩ?**
Usha:	**vo bas Draaiivar hãĩ. vo** Birmingham **mẽ rahte hãĩ. meraa chhoTaa bhaaii bhii** Birmingham **mẽ rahtaa hai. uskaa naam** Indresh **hai.**
Tarsem:	**vo kyaa kaam kartaa hai?**
Usha:	**vo dukaandaar hai.**
Tarsem:	**aapke kitne bachche hãĩ?**
Usha:	**hamaarii tiin beTiyãã hãĩ** – Rita, Anita, **aur** Sheela. Rita **aur** Anita secondary school **mẽ hãĩ. aur** Sheela primary school **mẽ hai.**

F

Christine:	**achchhaa, sabzii mẽ kyaa Daalte hãĩ?**
Manju:	**pyaaz, namak, lahsun aur TamaaTar.**
Christine:	**pyaaz, namak, lahsun aur TamaaTar . . . aapke paas hãĩ?**
Manju:	**pyaaz aur namak hãĩ . . . lahsun . . . mere paas lahsun nahĩĩ hai.**
Christine:	**kyaa aapko TamaaTar bhii chaahiyẽ?**
Manju:	**TamaaTar? jii hãã, mere paas TamaaTar bhii nahĩĩ hãĩ.**
Christine:	**achchhaa, aur kyaa Daalte hãĩ?**
Manju:	**sabzii mẽ aaluu bhii Daalte hãĩ, gaajar bhii Daalte hãĩ, paalak bhii Daalte hãĩ, aur dhaniyaa bhii Daalte hãĩ.**
Christine:	**aaluu, gaajar, paalak, aur dhaniyaa . . . kyaa aapko ye bhii chaahiyẽ?**
Manju:	**mujhe aaluu, paalak aur dhaniyaa chaahiyẽ . . . gaajarẽ mere paas hãĩ. mujhe gaajarẽ nahĩĩ chaahiyẽ.**

G

Christine:	ye kyaa hai?
Manju:	ye? ye sarsõ hai.
Christine:	sarsõ?
Manju:	hãã, sarsõ.
Christine:	sarsõ ko angrezii mē kyaa kahte hãĩ?
Manju:	Mustard.
Christine:	achchhaa, mustard. aur isko kyaa kahte hãĩ?
Manju:	muulii.
Christine:	muulii. isko kyaa karte hãĩ?
Manju:	isko salad mē Daalte hãĩ . . . achchhaa, muulii ko angrezii mē kyaa kahte hãĩ?
Christine:	angrezii mē isko radish kahte hãĩ.
Manju:	achchhaa, radish. aur usko kyaa kahte hãĩ?
Christine:	isko? . . . isko mint kahte hãĩ.
Manju:	Mint?
Christine:	hãã, mint ko hindii aur urduu mē kyaa kahte hãĩ?
Manju:	usko pudiinaa kahte hãĩ.

H

Waiter:	aaiye, ye aapkii mez hai. Menu liijiye saahab.
Ranjit:	shukriyaa. achchhaa aapko kyaa chaahiye, Jerry?
Jerry:	mujhe Rogan Josh chaahiye.
Ranjit:	ek Rogan Josh. Sandra aapko kyaa chaahiye?
Sandra:	biryaanii mē kyaa Daalte hãĩ?
Waiter:	chaaval, gosht, aur mirch-masaale.
Sandra:	Thiik hai. biryaanii kii ek pleT laaiye.
Waiter:	jii, Thiik hai.
Kamaljit:	mujhe bhii biryaanii chaahiye.
Ranjit:	Thiik hai. bhaaii saahab, Rogan Josh kii ek pleT, aur biryaanii kii do pleTē laaiye.
Waiter:	jii, aur aapko kyaa chaahiye?
Ranjit:	hãã, mujhe kyaa chaahiye? . . . kyaa aapke paas fish and chips hãĩ?
Waiter:	jii hãã.
Ranjit:	Thiik hai, fish and chips kii ek pleT laaiye.
Waiter:	jii, Thiik hai.

I

Shopkeeper:	assalaam alaikum.
Customer:	vaalaikum assalaam. kaise hãĩ?
Shopkeeper:	Thiik hũũ. aapko kyaa chaahiye?
Customer:	aaj mujhe aaluu chaahiyē.
Shopkeeper:	kitne paaunD?
Customer:	do.
Shopkeeper:	jii, aur kyaa chaahiye?
Customer:	gaajarē. mujhe chaar paaunD chaahiyē.
Shopkeeper:	Thiik hai.
Customer:	aur mujhe chaaval bhii chaahiyē.
Shopkeeper:	kitne?

Customer:	das paaunD.
Shopkeeper:	kyaa aapko muulii bhii chaahiye? aaj hamaare paas hai.
Customer:	jii nahĩĩ, aaj nahĩĩ chaahiye . . . achchhaa, aaluu, gaajar, aur chaaval. inkii Kiimat kyaa hai?
Shopkeeper:	aaluu – das pence ke ek paaunD. gaajarẽ – pandraa pence kii ek paaunD. chaaval – asii pence ke ek paaunD. aaTh paaunD asii pence.
Customer:	liijiye.
Shopkeeper:	shukriyaa.

J

Customer:	kyaa aapke paas paalak hai?
Shopkeeper:	jii hãã, baahar hai, dukaan ke saamne.
Customer:	achchhaa, mujhe methii bhii chaahiye. vo kahãã hai?
Shopkeeper:	methii bhii dukaan ke baahar hai, paalak ke paas.
Customer:	achchhaa Thiik hai. kyaa aapke paas muulii hai?
Shopkeeper:	jii hãã, yahãã dukaan ke andar hai, gaajarõ ke niiche.
Customer:	gaajarõ ke niiche? gaajarẽ kahãã hãĩ?
Shopkeeper:	vahãã, aapke piichhe.
Customer:	aapke piichhe?
Shopkeeper:	mere piichhe nahĩĩ, mere *saamne* hãĩ. *aapke* piichhe.
Customer:	achchhaa, achchhaa, *mere* piichhe. shukriyaa.
Shopkeeper:	aapko aur kyaa chaahiye?
Customer:	kyaa aapke paas pudiinaa aur sarsõ hãĩ?
Shopkeeper:	jii hãã, hãĩ.
Customer:	kahãã hãĩ?
Shopkeeper:	sarsõ baahar hai, methii aur paalak ke biich mẽ. aur pudiinaa yahãã andar hai, gaajarõ ke uupar.

UNIT 6

Doctor:	Hello jii, aap kaise hãĩ?
Patient 1:	Hello DaakTar saahab, mãĩ Thiik nahĩĩ hũũ.
Doctor:	kyaa baat hai?
Patient 1:	mere peT mẽ dard hai.
Doctor:	kal aapne kyaa khaayaa?
Patient 1:	kal mãĩne pulaav khaayaa. usmẽ kaafii mirch-masaale the.
Doctor:	kyaa aapko koii aur taKliif bhii hai?
Patient 1:	jii hãã, mujhe buKhaar bhii hai.

Doctor:	aap kaisii hãĩ?
Patient 2:	mãĩ Thiik nahĩĩ hũũ. kal mãĩ baahar gaii, aur mujhe sardii lagii.
Doctor:	kyaa aapko khããsii hai?
Patient 2:	jii hãã, meraa galaa Kharaab hai, aur mujhe sar-dard bhii hai.
Doctor:	kyaa aapko buKhaar bhii hai?
Patient 2:	jii nahĩĩ.

Doctor:	namaste.
Patient 3:	namaste.
Doctor:	aap kaisii hãĩ?
Patient 3:	mujhe buKhaar hai.

Doctor:	kyaa aapko sardii lagii hai?
Patient 3:	jii nahĩĩ. kal mujhe thoRii khããsii thii. meraa galaa bhii Kharaab thaa, magar aaj nahĩĩ hai.
Doctor:	kyaa kal aapne khaanaa khaayaa?
Patient 3:	jii nahĩĩ, mere peT mẽ dard thaa, magar aaj peT bhii Thiik hai.
Doctor:	achchhaa, kyaa aapko koii aur taKliif bhii hai?
Patient 3:	jii, mujhe thoRaa sar-dard bhii hai.

UNIT 7

A

meraa naam Ann Lawson hai. mãĩ Tiichar hũũ. mãĩ Rochdale mẽ rahtii hũũ aur Bolton mẽ kaam kartii hũũ. mãĩ tiin saal se urduu siikh rahii hũũ. mãĩ urduu paRh bhii saktii hũũ aur thoRii likh bhii saktii hũũ. mãĩ hindii bhii bol saktii hũũ magar paRh nahĩĩ saktii.

B

meraa naam Rowshon Malik hai. mãĩ Tower Hamlets mẽ rahtii bhii hũũ aur kaam bhii kartii hũũ. mãĩ vahãã DaakTar hũũ. ghar mẽ mãĩ Bengali boltii hũũ, magar ab mãĩ ek saal se hindii aur urduu siikh rahii hũũ. hindii mãĩ paRh bhii saktii hũũ, likh bhii saktii hũũ, magar urduu mẽ apnaa naam hii likh saktii hũũ.

C

meraa naam Abdul Rahim (abdul rahiim) hai. skuul mẽ mere Tiichar ne mujhe kaafii urduu sikhaa dii thii. mãĩ urduu bol saktaa hũũ, paRh bhii saktaa hũũ, aur likh bhii saktaa hũũ. ab mãĩ Nottingham mẽ rahtaa hũũ. mãĩ yahãã librarian hũũ, aur do saal se hindii siikh rahaa hũũ. mãĩne kaafii hindii siikh lii hai, aur ab mãĩ hindii kii kitaabẽ bhii paRh saktaa hũũ.

UNIT 8

Sneh:	aapko Play Punjabi kaa gaanaa Bhangra Bash kaisaa lagtaa hai?
Punter 1:	mujhe bahut achchhaa lagtaa hai. mujhe bhangRaa bahut pasand hai.
Sneh:	kyaa aapko Bhangra Bash pasand hai?
Punter 2:	jii nahĩĩ, mujhe pasand nahĩĩ hai.
Sneh:	aapko Bhangra Bash kaisaa lagtaa hai?
Punter 3:	mujhe achchhaa lagtaa hai.
Sneh:	kyaa aapko Play Punjabi kaa Bhangra Bash pasand hai?
Punter 4:	jii hãã, bahut pasand hai.
Sneh:	kyaa aapko bhangra music sunne kaa shauK hai?
Punter 5:	jii hãã.
Sneh:	achchhaa, aapko Play Punjabi kaa Bhangra Bash kaisaa lagtaa hai?
Punter 5:	bahut buraa lagtaa hai.
Sneh:	aapko Bhangra Bash kaisaa lagtaa hai?
Punter 6:	mujhe bahut pasand hai.
Sneh:	kyaa aapko Bhangra Bash pasand hai?
Punter 7:	jii nahĩĩ, pasand nahĩĩ hai.
Sneh:	kyaa aapko Play Punjabi kaa gaanaa Bhangra Bash pasand hai?
Punter 8:	jii nahĩĩ. unko gaanaa gaanaa nahĩĩ aataa.

Sneh:	**kyaa aapko** Bhangra Bash **achchhaa lagtaa hai?**
Punter 9:	**jii hā̃, kaafii achchhaa lagtaa hai.**
Sneh:	**aapko** Play Punjabi **kaa** Bhangra Bash **achchhaa yaa buraa lagtaa hai?**
Punter 10:	**buraa to nahī̃ lagtaa . . . magar bahut achchhaa bhii nahī̃ lagtaa.**

UNIT 9

Travel agent:	**aapko kahā̃ jaanaa hai?**
Traveller 1:	**mā̃i** India **jaanaa chaahtaa hū̃u.**
Travel agent:	**kab jaanaa chaahte hā̃i?**
Traveller 1:	December **mē̃.**
Travel Agent:	**kyaa aap havaaii jahaaz se jaanaa chaahte hā̃i?**
Traveller 1:	**jii hā̃.**
Travel agent:	**kyaa aapko dillii jaanaa hai, yaa** Bombay **(bambaii)?**
Traveller 1:	Bombay, **aur** Bombay **se mā̃i** Madras **(madraas) jaaū̃ugaa.**
Travel agent:	Madras **kaise jaaēge?**
Traveller 1:	**Tren mē̃.**
Travel agent:	**agar aap havaaii jahaaz se jaaē to kam vaKt lagegaa.**
Traveller 1:	**jii hā̃, magar mere paas vaKt bahut hai. mā̃i Tren mē̃ hii jaaū̃ugaa.**
Travel agent:	**aap kahā̃ jaanaa chaahtii hā̃i?**
Traveller 2:	**mā̃i** Rawalpindi **jaanaa chaahtii hū̃u. kaise jaa saktii hū̃u?**
Travel agent:	**aap havaaii jahaaz se islaamaabaad tak jaa saktii hā̃i. vahā̃ se aapko** Rawalpindi **bas mē̃ yaa Tren mē̃ jaanaa hogaa. agar aap bas mē̃ jaaē to kam vaKt lagegaa.**
Traveller 2:	**Thiik hai. mā̃i aise hii karū̃ugii.**
Travel agent:	**aap vahā̃ kab jaaēgii?**
Traveller 2:	**mā̃i janvarii mē̃ jaanaa chaahtii hū̃u.**
Travel agent:	**mā̃i aapke liye kyaa kar saktaa hū̃u?**
Traveller 3:	**mujhe do TikTē chaahiyē. mujhe** Kenya **jaanaa hai.**
Travel agent:	**aapko kab jaanaa hai?**
Traveller 3:	November **mē̃.** Nairobi **tak ham havaaii jahaaz se jaaēge, magar ham** Mombassa **bhii jaanaa chaahte hā̃i.** Nairobi **se** Mombassa **kaise jaaē?**
Travel agent:	Mombassa **aap Tren mē̃ bhii, aur havaaii jahaaz se bhii jaa sakte hā̃i. mere Khayaal mē̃ aap havaaii jahaaz se jaaē.**
Traveller 3:	**Thiik hai. ham aise hii karēge.**

UNIT 10

meraa naam Jay Prakash **(jay prakaash) hai. mā̃i** Preston **mē̃ rahtaa hū̃u,** number 10, High Street **par. mā̃i** India **mē̃ paidaa huaa thaa, aur merii paRhaaii bhii** India **mē̃ hii huii. mere skuul kaa naam** Salwan Boys' Upper Secondary School **thaa. vo dillii mē̃ hai. jab mā̃i aThaaraa saal kaa thaa tab mā̃i yahā̃ is mulk mē̃ aayaa. yahā̃ aakar mā̃ine sab se pahle** machine operator **kaa kaam kiyaa. uske baad mā̃i** bus driver **ban gayaa, aur ab mā̃i dukaandaar hū̃u.**

meraa naam Vijay Singh **hai, aur mā̃i** Punjab **(panjaab) mē̃ paidaa huaa thaa. ab mā̃i** Blackburn **mē̃** number 92, Manchester Rd **par rahtaa hū̃u. merii koii paRhaaii nahī̃ huii, aur jab mā̃i biis saal kaa thaa tab mā̃i yahā̃ aayaa. yahā̃ aakar mā̃ine** restaurant **mē̃ kaam karnaa**

shuruu kiyaa, aur tab se aaj tak maĩ restaurants mē hii kaam kar rahaa hũũ.

meraa naam Feroze Khan (firoz Khaan) hai. maĩ 297 Stratford Rd par rahtaa hũũ, Birmingham mē. jab maĩ is mulk mē aayaa tab merii umr pandraa saal kii thii. yahãã aakar maĩ Birmingham ke Steward's Centre School gayaa. vahãã maĩne thoRii angrezii siikh lii. uske baad maĩne restaurant mē waiter kaa kaam kiyaa. phir maĩ taxi driver ban gayaa. ab maĩne restaurant Khariid liyaa hai aur apnaa kaarobaar shuruu kar liyaa hai.